DIGITAL FORENSICS
TRIAL GRAPHICS

DIGITAL FORENSICS TRIAL GRAPHICS

Teaching the Jury through Effective Use of Visuals

JOHN SAMMONS

LARS DANIEL

ACADEMIC PRESS

An imprint of Elsevier
elsevier.com

Academic Press is an imprint of Elsevier
125 London Wall, London EC2Y 5AS, United Kingdom
525 B Street, Suite 1800, San Diego, CA 92101-4495, United States
50 Hampshire Street, 5th Floor, Cambridge, MA 02139, United States
The Boulevard, Langford Lane, Kidlington, Oxford OX5 1GB, United Kingdom

Notices
Knowledge and best practice in this field are constantly changing. As new research and
experience broaden our understanding, changes in research methods, professional practices,
or medical treatment may become necessary.

Practitioners and researchers must always rely on their own experience and knowledge
in evaluating and using any information, methods, compounds, or experiments described
herein. In using such information or methods they should be mindful of their own safety
and the safety of others, including parties for whom they have a professional responsibility.

To the fullest extent of the law, neither the Publisher nor the authors, contributors, or
editors, assume any liability for any injury and/or damage to persons or property as a
matter of products liability, negligence or otherwise, or from any use or operation of any
methods, products, instructions, or ideas contained in the material herein.

Library of Congress Cataloging-in-Publication Data
A catalog record for this book is available from the Library of Congress

British Library Cataloguing-in-Publication Data
A catalogue record for this book is available from the British Library

ISBN: 978-0-12-803483-5

For information on all Academic Press publications visit our
website at https://www.elsevier.com/books-and-journals

Working together
to grow libraries in
developing countries

www.elsevier.com • www.bookaid.org

Publisher: Sara Tenney
Acquisition Editor: Elizabeth Brown
Editorial Project Manager: Anna Valutkevich
Production Project Manager: Priya Kumaraguruparan
Cover Designer: Mark Rogers

Typeset by TNQ Books and Journals

*For Lora, Abby, and Rae for making me a truly blessed and lucky man.
To my aunt Ruth whose love, support, and encouragement mean so much. To my
mother Juanita, and my grandmother Grace, for the many sacrifices you made and
the example you set...I miss you.*

—John Sammons

*I dedicate this book to my wife, Destiny: Always and forever the
apple of my eye.*

—Lars Daniel

CONTENTS

ABOUT THE AUTHORS

John Sammons is an associate professor and Director of the undergraduate program in Digital Forensics and Information Assurance at Marshall University in Huntington, West Virginia. John teaches digital forensics, electronic discovery, information security, and technology in the School of Forensic and Criminal Justices Sciences. He is also adjunct faculty with the Marshall University graduate forensic science program where he teaches the advanced digital forensics course. John, a former police officer, is also an investigator with the Cabell County Prosecuting Attorney's Office and a member of the West Virginia Internet Crimes Against Children Task Force. He is a member of the American Academy of Forensic Sciences, the High Technology Crime Investigation Association, and InfraGard.

John is the founder and President of the Appalachian Institute of Digital Evidence. AIDE is a nonprofit organization that provides research and training for digital evidence professionals including attorneys, judges, and law enforcement and information security practitioners in the private sector. He is the author of best-selling book, *The Basics of Digital Forensics* published by Syngress.

Lars Daniel is a digital forensics examiner at Guardian Digital Forensics.

Lars is an EnCase Certified Examiner, an AccessData Certified Examiner, an AccessData Certified Mobile Examiner, a Certified Telecommunications Network Specialist, Certified Wireless Analyst, a Certified Internet Protocol Telecommunications Specialist, and a Certified Telecommunications Analyst.

He spoke at the largest annual digital forensics conference, the Computer Enterprise and Investigations Conference, in 2011 and 2013 and at the EnFuse Conference in 2016.

Lars has qualified as an expert witness and testified in both state and federal court qualifying as a digital forensics expert, computer forensics expert, a cell phone forensics expert, a video forensics expert, and a photo forensics expert.

He has attended over 300 h of forensic training and has worked on over 600 cases involving murder, child pornography, terrorism, rape, kidnapping, intellectual property, fraud, wrongful death, employee wrongdoing, and insurance losses among numerous other types of cases.

Lars is the coauthor of the book *Digital Forensics for Legal Professionals: Understanding Digital Evidence from the Warrant to the Courtroom*, published by Syngress, an imprint of Elsevier Publishing.

He has extensive experience in both civil and criminal defense cases. He provides continuing legal education training classes for attorneys across the United States.

FOREWORD

Digital Forensics Trial Graphics
Teaching the Jury Though Effective Use of Visuals
John Sammons and Lars Daniel

In reality, this book is may be improperly subtitled; perhaps it should read, "Teaching everyone through effective use of visuals."

What John Sammons and Lars Daniel have done with *Digital Forensics Trial Graphics* is to boil down the essentials of good graphic design into a few impactful chapters. They have not bogged down the content with too much detail, after all, this book is for practicing digital forensics experts, not for art students.

As an expert in any field, but especially in the extremely technical world of digital forensics, communicating complex technical information to a layperson is one of the most challenging and yet rewarding services we perform. And when I say layperson, I am including everyone who may be involved in a legal situation, be it a criminal trial or a civil action. Judges, police, attorneys, and jurors all fall into the category of layperson when confronted by technical evidence of the sort that we as digital forensics experts deal with everyday.

As you will see in this book, easy for us experts to treat our well of knowledge as commonplace since we understand the jargon and can effortlessly bat about acronyms like verbal badminton birdies.

Consider the last time you went to your physician for a visit. Did you understand everything she/he said, or did that medical term confound you? Did you ask her/him to explain what the heck that term meant? Or did you leave knowing less than you should have about whatever medical issue that drove you to make that visit to the doctor in the first place?

It is easy to forget that the people we are charged with conveying our knowledge to, the triers of fact, a.k.a the jurors, are not allowed to ask questions. They are totally dependent on our ability to convey complex technical information to them so they can consider that information in making what could be a life or death decision.

In our profession, strong communication skills, especially the ability to reduce complexity to simplicity in creating reports and presentations that will be provided to jurors and others in a courtroom, is a critical skill that cannot be ignored if we are to be the experts we need to be.

We spend a lot of time perfecting our skills in the area of digital forensics by pursuing training specific to our field. Nothing in that training prepares us to create the kind of visual aids we need to teach what we know to someone completely unfamiliar with our field. What most people think they know about digital forensics comes from watching "Hollywood forensics" in television programs such as CSI.

It is our job and our obligation to put forward the best explanation of what a juror needs to understand in the most effective form possible. Trial graphics are one of the ways we can accomplish that goal.

Over the years I have worked with Lars Daniel to create and present digital forensics concepts to thousands of attorneys, judges, law enforcement, and others involved in the legal profession through continuing legal education classes.

Between his experience and mine, we have presented expert testimony in state and federal courts over 75 times. This experience is invaluable in understanding how laypersons perceive and grasp the concepts in digital forensics. And his experience is evident in this book.

What I appreciate most about Sammons and Daniel's *Digital Forensics Trial Graphics* is that it guides the reader through the process of understanding how graphics should be designed and used to communicate.

They have effectively stripped away all but the meat of the subject. This makes the idea of learning "graphic design" for the technical crowd much less daunting that picking up an art design book and starting from scratch.

They have levered their personal expertise and their scholarly backgrounds to produce a book that is both approachable and practical.

After working in this field for 16 years, I find it remarkable that none of the university digital forensics programs include a course dealing with this subject.

I can say without reservation that this book, and more specifically, the methods it espouses, has changed my life for the better. Even after all the years I have spent in this field, having access to *Digital Forensics Trial Graphics* has opened my eyes to new and better ways to approach communicating with juries.

And communicating our findings is the purpose of what we do.

Larry E. Daniel
Digital Forensics Examiner and Cellular Analyst
Guardian Digital Forensics
Raleigh, NC, October 2016

CHAPTER ONE

Introduction

Abstract

Communication is an integral part of our everyday lives. In a courtroom, effective communication is the most important skill you can have. The ability to teach the jury about
your evidence and case will drive the outcome of your case. Using visual communication is one of the best ways to teach people about new information and help them
understand and retain that information. Knowing how to prepare and present your
case using visual communication will be the focus of this book.

Keywords: Jury; Presentation; Presenting evidence; Visual communication; Visuals.

If we can convert an idea into an image, we should do so

James Zull (2002).

Humans are highly visual creatures. Approximately half of the human brain
is directly (or indirectly) devoted to our sense of vision (Weinschenk, 2012).
There is no doubt that visual communication is highly effective. Pictures
make things both easier to understand and to remember. For example,
research indicates you'll only remember about 10% of information you
hear after 3 days. Adding a picture will make that number jump substantially
to 65% (Medina, 2014).

Clearly there's a need to leverage the power of visuals in communication.
The problem is that there is a significant knowledge gap when it comes to
visual communication. Think about how much time you've spent in school
learning to communicate with written and spoken language. We started at a
very young age learning rules of grammar, vocabulary, and proper spelling.
That study and practice literally span all levels of education, from elemen-
tary school through graduate studies at a university. Now compare that to
the time you spent learning how to communicate visually. The difference is
astronomical. Why is the commitment to learning visual communication so
disproportionate despite its proven effectiveness? That's a great question and
people are starting to raise it.

Digital Forensics Trial Graphics
ISBN 978-0-12-803483-5
http://dx.doi.org/10.1016/B978-0-12-803483-5.00001-3

George Lucas (yes, that George Lucas) is a very strong advocate of teaching visual communication in schools. Lucas is a firm believer in the power of visuals in communication. When asked by a reporter what's at stake if this understanding doesn't make its way into the classroom, Lucas replied:

> You're already seeing it. You often see very educated people—doctors and lawyers and engineers—trying to make presentations, and they have no clue about how to communicate visually and what happens when you put one image after another. So their lectures become very confused because, from a visual perspective, they're putting their periods at the front of their sentences, and nobody understands them....Understanding these rules is as important as learning how to make a sentence work
>
> **Daly (2004).**

At its core, this is a book about communication. Communication in the context of a court of law. More specifically, it's a book that will teach you how to effectively use visuals to communicate your knowledge and expertise to a jury in a way that isn't intimidating or hard to understand. We'll show you how using proper visuals will make both your job and the juries' job much easier. In the book's remaining six chapters, we'll cover the theory and practice of creating and using visuals to significantly enhance your courtroom testimony.

CHAPTER 2: BUT I AM NOT AN ARTIST

Right from the start it's very important to understand that what you trying to create isn't a work of art. You certainly don't need to be Da Vinci to create an effective slide deck that really helps the jury. Sure, they may be eye pleasing but that should never be the yardstick you use to measure the real value of your visuals. A well-done visual doesn't have to be a work of art. The objective isn't to awe the jury with a beautiful masterpiece but rather to provide them a mechanism by which they can learn and remember the information you deliver. An excellent visual is less about the visual itself and more about how it helps you move the jury from a point of little or no understanding to a point of understanding that's helpful to them in their decision making process.

As an expert witness, it's all too easy to forget what it's like not to know what you know. Concepts and ideas that seem simple and easy to understand for you will likely be complicated and confusing to a jury. The purpose of a visual aid is to break down this complex information and make it easier to understand. When preparing your testimony, it's important to remember that the final product shouldn't be "flashy" PowerPoint slides packed with bullets and text.

Illustrations are a powerful tool that will allow you to break down complex technical information into simple, understandable information the jury can use. Any illustration you use should be simple and to the point. It should serve a purpose.

CHAPTER 3: PRINCIPLES OF GRAPHIC DESIGN: THE BASICS

In Chapter 3, you will start to examine some basic "visual grammar" you can use when designing and developing the visual aspects of your testimony. Using these basic principles will help you create visual aids that will enhance your testimony and help you get the most out of your design. The chapter focuses on four basic design principles: contrast, alignment, repetition, and proximity (CARP for short).

Contrast creates visual interest and helps the viewer connect information while emphasizes its unique qualities. Contrast can be visualized using tone, color, size, shape, and texture. Tone utilizes dark and light to emphasize contrast. Color enhances the visual and holds the viewer's attention. Size guides the viewer down a particular path in the visual, moving them from one point to another. Shape can create a "feeling" about the information before facts about the information are presented. Texture can create a sensation for the viewer about certain information without them having to touch or feel it.

Alignment is critical in creating a cohesive visual aid. It creates a visual system that allows the viewer to identify individual elements and see how they connect to each other.

Repetition will increase the viewer's likelihood to remember and connect new information. It also helps to create a feeling of cohesiveness in your presentation.

Proximity also creates visual unity in your visual aid and helps the viewer see how information relates to each other.

A sure sign of a great graphic or slide design is when the design elements themselves disappear, allowing the jurors to focus on what matters the most, the content. The juror shouldn't be thinking about the design of the slide but rather the information it is relaying. It's our responsibility to leverage the power of visuals to enhance jury learning, understanding, and retention so that they can use our evidence to reach an accurate verdict.

CHAPTER 4: SLIDE DESIGN: BEST PRACTICES

Chapter 4 covers the best practices you'll want to employ when designing and developing your slides and slide deck.

Typically, the evidence we are asked to testify about is highly technical. The overwhelming majority of jurors we encounter can be quickly overwhelmed with jargon, acronyms, and technology. Realistically, the jury is only going to be able to remember the fundamentals of any technical explanation we make. Proper executed visuals can go a long way in making our testimony accessible, even to the most "technology-challenged" juror on the panel.

Start planning your slide presentation on paper instead of diving right into the presentation software. This "analogue" approach allows you to focus directly on the actual content rather than seeing it through the function and features of the software. At the beginning, it's imperative that you understand the scope of your testimony, the key pieces of evidence, the technical concepts that need to be explained, and the audience that you'll be explaining it to.

When it comes to slide design, it's nearly impossible to overemphasize the need for simplicity. Simplicity is critical if we have any hope in getting the jury to really understand and retain the evidence we present. Simplicity, however, is tough to achieve. It requires a lot of hard work and thought to really achieve. It's important that the jury not only understand your testimony, but that they retain it as well. Building repetition into your slide deck of the key pieces of information will help with retention.

Cut any and all extraneous elements and information from your slides and slide deck. Strip out any word, image, or concept that isn't absolutely necessary. The best advice is usually "cut and then cut some more." Remember that the slide is there for the jury, not for you. Commit the time and energy into producing simple, quality visuals that support and enhance your testimony.

The theory that "less is more" in more holds true for many things including slide design. When building slides, we should always be thinking about cutting text, images, and other elements rather than adding them.

In keeping with the "less is more" theme, there are several things you should avoid including the following:
- Complete sentences
- More than two to three colors

- More than two fonts
- More than one kind of subtle animation
- Tons of information crammed onto a single slide

When you're building slides, avoid the common traps that many people fall into, namely bullet points. We've all seen lousy PowerPoint presentations, which are often characterized by their bullet-laden slides. Bullet points are overused and are boring. If you must use them, do so sparingly.

You should use only quality graphics and images in your slides and avoid using cheesy clip art. You should also make sure your words and images are working together by sending the same message. Lastly, the chapter explores the proper use of charts and graphs.

CHAPTER 5: PRESENTING FOR COMPREHENSION

As an expert witness, you need to embrace your role as a teacher in the courtroom. Just like a teacher, your objective is to move the jurors through very complex information, to a place of understanding and comprehension. Despite your best efforts, even the most invested and interested juror is only likely to understand and retain a small amount of the evidence you present.

The type of language you use matters, especially to the jury. It's easy for you to overwhelm them with jargon and technical terms. But, since jurors often rely heavily on the scientific or technical evidence you present, it's critical that you do the heavy lifting, making your testimony accessible to them.

Studies have shown that people learn best when new information is tied or connected to information they already know. This is especially true with very complex material. As an expert witness you'll have better success at teaching the jury if you're able to tie very technical concepts to common things that most people already know. Analogies and stories are great tools you can use to do this. When you're designing your visuals, keep this principle in mind.

CHAPTER 6: PUTTING IT ALL TOGETHER

Chapter 6: Putting It All Together examines a real word case and the graphics that were used to educate the jury.

CHAPTER 7: PREPARING GRAPHICS FOR PRODUCTION

This chapter will explore the benefits and constraints of each medium as well as some of the graphic design tools available to help create your visual aids. This chapter also offers advice on preparing graphics for production based on real-life courtroom experiences.

In choosing your medium it's important to remember that your goal is to relay evidence in a clear/concise way without the type of medium distracting from your presentation.

You'll either present your testimony with print or digital medium. There are benefits and constraints to both mediums. Visuals in a digital format are easy to transport and a large amount of data can be contained in a small space. The downside to digital is that it's dependent on technology that doesn't always work or isn't always available.

Printed visuals can be more dependable, but they are bulky to transport and hard to correct after they are printed. In addition, printed visuals can be made available to every jury member. As a general rule it's a good idea to have a print copy of any digital presentation as a backup.

REFERENCES

Daly, J. (September 14, 2004). *Life on the screen: Visual literacy in education*. Retrieved from Edutopia: http://www.edutopia.org/life-screen.

Medina, J. (2014). *Brain rules*. Seattle, WA: Pear Press. Retrieved from: http://www.brainrules.net/vision.

Weinschenk, S. (2012). *100 things every presenter needs to know about people*. New Riders.

Zull, J. E. (2002). *The art of changing the brain: Enriching the practice of teaching by exploring the biology of learning*. Sterling: Stylus Publishing.

CHAPTER TWO

But I Am Not an Artist

Contents

Abstract

The purpose of this chapter is to ensure the reader that this book with help them to better communicate by creating and using visuals, even if they have the artistic talent of a tree stump.

Keywords: Artist; Digital forensics; Graphic design; Tools.

Information in this chapter:

- It doesn't matter if you are an artist, anyone can make good graphics.
- Turning expertise into illustration is the primary goal.

INTRODUCTION

If you ever had an art class in grade school or college, then you know that one person who could draw anything they laid eyes on with astounding precision, or the person who could paint a landscape that made you feel the Sun on your face and dew glistening grass underfoot. Well, for the vast majority of us, we are not blessed with the artistic prowess of a Michelangelo or Rembrandt. But that's ok.

A well–done visual does not have to be a stunningly beautiful one. Excellent visuals aren't about the visuals themselves, but about how the visual helps the audience to better understand a particular subject. Luckily for us, a simple and

Digital Forensics Trial Graphics
ISBN 978-0-12-803483-5
http://dx.doi.org/10.1016/B978-0-12-803483-5.00002-5

well-planned visual can communicate information as good as a gorgeous one. In fact, sometimes simple is better. Just as someone can get lost in the transcendent prose of a wordsmith, so they can also miss the forest for the trees if the visual is more about conveying its own beauty than actually explaining a subject.

The whole purpose of visuals within the context of this book is to take complicated technical concepts and explain them in an easily understandable way. With this as our goal, we will examine in this chapter what our mind-set and priorities should be as a digital forensics examiner playing the part of a graphic artist, and not the other way around.

EXPERTISE INTO ILLUSTRATION

I have had times when I was struggling with a difficult concept, and an illustration truly made the difference in my understanding that concept or not. That is what we are attempting to provide with these illustrations. Our goal is to act as translators of our expertise into an approachable illustration that assists a layperson.

Sometimes when you speak with someone who is an expert in their field it can be quite daunting, and this is particularly true if this is an area where you have little to no knowledge. In all likelihood, the expert is not trying to confuse you or to obfuscate the information, but instead the body of water between the shore of his/her knowledge and yours is simply too far to cross. Many of us have had this experience with a professor in college, where subjects were taught as if they are as simple as day, but to the students it is like learning alien hieroglyphics.

It is important to remember that as an expert, you take much of your knowledge for granted. When explaining anything, whether it is through language, an illustration, or both, try to remember back when you were a novice at your discipline. If you could go back in time and explain to yourself a difficult technical concept you struggled with then, how would you do it? I bet that explanation wouldn't be laden with acronyms, jargon, or geek speak. You would probably try to find something every person can relate to and use that to explain the concept, to find common ground with the younger you, and use that as a launching pad to explain the concept.

Even seemingly simple questions can sometimes become quite daunting when you think about trying to translate it to a layperson. For example, even if we take a simple question such as "how does a computer organize data?" it takes serious thought to decide where to start.

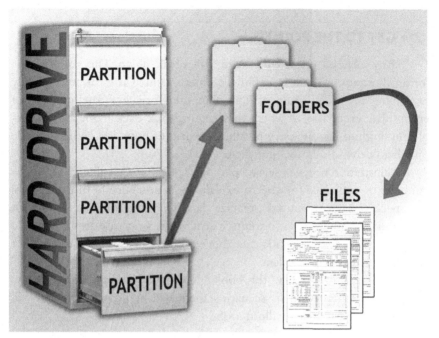

Figure 2.1

With a layperson, starting with operating systems, file systems, or the difference between a hard drive and a solid state drive is almost assuredly not the right place. Remember, you have to assume that your audience has only the most basic knowledge of the technology you are explaining.

Maybe a better place to start is with something everyone has experience with; like a filing cabinet. Take a look at Fig. 2.1. You can explain how a computer stores data on a hard drive as a filing cabinet, with drawers, folders, and files. The cabinet itself would be the hard drive; each of the drawers in the cabinet would be a partition or volume, with each partition containing folders and the folders containing files.

So if you explained this in the courtroom, using the illustration as your guide, you could explain it like this:

Think of your hard drive as a filing cabinet, and each of the drawers inside the cabinet are partitions (or volumes). If you have ever seen your C drive or D drive on a computer, these are volumes. Inside the volume, are folders. Folders would consist of your My Documents, Pictures, and Downloads folders. Inside of these folders are individual files, such as the pictures from your vacation.

GET TO THE POINT

Any analogy pressed too hard will break down. The same is true for an illustration. While our filing cabinet example is great at efficiently explaining the architecture of how computers organize data, it does not encapsulate every way in which they can organize data, and it is not complex enough to handle every possible scenario of how data come to reside on a hard drive and how it got there.

An illustration needs to serve a particular purpose. One illustration is not going to be sufficient for you to explain to an audience both the general and specific ways computers organize data. The filing cabinet is great for general understanding, but if forensic artifacts in your case are related to a particular type of very specific data, then you need a custom illustration that can properly explain that data.

While the illustrations in this book and others will be provided to you, and will be useful for many scenarios, there will be times when you will need to make very specific illustrations.

BUILDING BLOCKS

The cornerstone of making good illustrations is turning complicated technical concepts into easily understood information. Now that we have set that stone, let's look as some of the building blocks that will assist us in reaching that goal.

Basics of Design

An understanding of how to design effective graphics will be reinforced throughout the book, both explicitly in Chapter 4: Principles of Graphic Design, and implicitly throughout the rest of the book.

Assisting you in understanding good design is one of the goals of this book, but it is not necessary for you to become an artist. I do not need to know the science behind the internal combustion engine to change an oil filter, and likewise, you do not need to know every facet of design to become proficient in making good graphics.

Graphic Design Tools

Choosing the appropriate graphic design tools is a key building block. You will not need to master a plethora of tools, and this does not require a significant financial investment. In fact, it is likely that you already have tools that can be used to make good graphics such as Microsoft Word.

There will be discussion throughout the book related to various graphic design tools, ranging from free tools, common software programs that can be used as graphic design tools, all the way to professional level programs for those so inclined. For an outline of some of the more common tools, see Appendix A: Choosing Graphic Design Software.

SUMMARY

It is important that we don't miss the forest for the trees. That is why in this chapter we start with the why, and not with the how. Remember as you read this book that talk about good design, graphics programs, or how to get your images ready for PowerPoint or print are all secondary. The prime mover is always translating complicated technical concepts so that they can be understood by everyone in the room.

CHAPTER THREE

Principles of Graphic Design: The Basics

Contents

Abstract

This chapter will act as a primer for the new student of graphic design or a helpful refresher to a more experienced practitioner on design basics, specifically as it relates to creating useful graphics for presenting information.

Keywords: CARP; Contrast; Graphic design; Illustrations; Principles of design.

Information in this chapter:

- The basic.s of graphic design
- How to use CARP as a set of guidelines

INTRODUCTION

Even if you have never studied the principles of design before, I can just about guarantee that you can tell the difference between good design and bad design. In this chapter, we will examine the foundations of what makes good design.

Digital Forensics Trial Graphics
ISBN 978-0-12-803483-5
http://dx.doi.org/10.1016/B978-0-12-803483-5.00003-7

When you are giving an explanation it is often helpful, if not completely necessary, to explain both what you do mean, and what you do not mean so that your audience can truly understand your position. In that same vein, we will look at examples of good design and bad design in this chapter so that you can both identify the specific differences and have the tools to fix poor design.

CONTRAST, ALIGNMENT, REPETITION, PROXIMITY

No, we are not talking about a fish. Contrast, alignment, repetition, proximity (CARP) is the acronym used by designers as shorthand for the four design principles of contrast, alignment, repetition, and proximity. Remember, these are the very core principles. There are many other aspects of design, and volumes have been written about all of them. Our goal is to get the maximum return for our effort, and CARP will allow us to do just that as we apply these principles to our very specific goal of digital forensics trial graphics.

CONTRAST

Is a power line utility pole tall? That is a tough question to answer without contrasting it to something else. Compared to my height, sure it is tall; compared to the Empire State Building, not so much.

Contrast is about more than just color or size. Contrast, just as with language, is used in graphic arts to show the uniqueness of dissimilar things or ideas. Contrast is important to create visual interest in a graphic. If a design lacks contrast it is likely the audience will become visually disinterested sooner. This may seem unimportant for technical illustrations, but this is not the case.

Remember, we are attempting to make graphics that are useful for nontechnical people who are inundated with graphics everyday from billboards during their daily commute, when checking their Facebook page, to every packaged food product purchased from the grocery store.

Attention spans are a limited resource, so our graphics need to utilize contrast to make our graphics visually appealing and engaging (Fig. 3.1).

Utilizing Contrast in Graphic Design

If you have ever shopped for a diamond, then it is likely you have seen the persuasive powers of contrast put to use. A good jeweler, whether he or she knows it or not, is an expert in contrast. As we explain contrast in further details, we will examine why this is.

Figure 3.1 If someone asked you to describe this picture, the elements of contrast give you many tools to explain the differences in size, shape, color, and even the texture because of the differing types of fur. It is unlikely an onlooker would describe this picture as simply being "an image of two dogs" given all of the visual interest.

Contrast: Tone

The jeweler pulls the diamond from the case. He/she then places that diamond on a black velvet cloth. That diamond will sparkle and glisten the same on a white cloth just as it would on a black cloth, but the contrast between the blackness of that velvet cloth and that shining diamond allows you to see the properties of that diamond in much greater detail. The contrast in tone, darkness, and lightness captures the attention (Fig. 3.2).

Contrast: Color

You have selected a diamond, and to your eye it looks clear and white. You feel comfortable with your selection and are on the cusp of purchasing it. Well, the jeweler knows that if you look at that diamond side by side with a higher grade of diamond that it will look cloudy and yellow (Fig. 3.3).

Figure 3.2 When looking at these three diamonds, notice how your eye is drawn to the diamond on the black background. This is the power of contrasting tone; the dark next to the light creates interest to the eyes.

Figure 3.3 It can be difficult to illustrate contrast in color in a black and white book. But, we have all seen a rainbow, and what makes a rainbow visually stunning is the clearly delineated lines of color. You can also think of the beauty of a sunset, with the gradient of blue-black blending into orange and then a smoky red. Nature has many such examples of stunning color contrasts.

Contrast: Size

You've gone into the store set on purchasing a 1/2 carat diamond ring. You examine the ring on mannequin hands and it sure looks great, plenty big enough in your mind. Well, this is where the jeweler uses the power of comparison once again. That 1/2 carat diamond looks plenty large in isolation, but when compared to a 1 carat diamond it looks small, and compared to anything 2 carats or larger it looks downright miniscule (Figs. 3.4–3.6).

Contrast: Shape

Round, princess, pear, cushion, heart, asscher, oval, emerald, marquise, and radiant: Yes, it sounds like I am naming magic ponies in a children's show, but these are just some of the shapes diamonds come in. You may come into the store only interested in round diamonds, but that jeweler knows that the longer they keep you in the store, the better the chance they will make a sale. The variety created by contrasting shapes are likely to keep you engaged for longer than row upon row of round diamonds.

If contrasting shapes were unimportant we would all drive cars that maximize efficiency in a wind tunnel and not visual appeal. We would all live in efficiency-shaped box houses lacking any architectural detail, and decorate our homes with unadorned minimalist furniture.

Figure 3.4 Contrasting the size of objects in a design can be used for many purposes. It is often used in humor. Think of the clown with the giant shoes, a huge man walking a tiny dog.

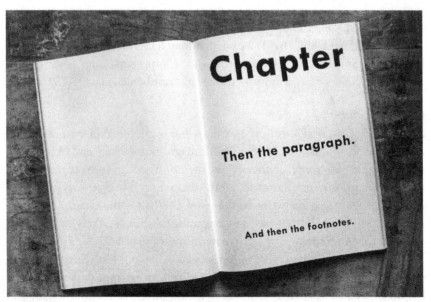

Figure 3.5 Contrasting size can also be used as a visual roadmap for your viewer. Think of how the typography in books is designed in a hierarchal fashion, from larger to smaller. You start at a chapter (largest), which leads you to the main body of writing, and then you have footnotes in tiny text at the bottom, telling your eyes where to start and where to finish.

Figure 3.6 We use contrasting size everyday to determine even the most mundane tasks, such as picking the correct door to enter. In this illustration, it is much easier to tell which door is the front door on the rightmost house versus the left.

Figure 3.7 The different shapes that make up the faces of these cars give the viewer cues about the intended purpose and audience of these vehicles.

Contrasting shapes have the ability to give the viewer a feeling about something before they know any factual information about it. Think of the glowering face of a muscle car, all chrome teeth and downturned grill versus the smiley design and perky headlights of a hybrid family hatchback (Fig. 3.7).

Contrast: Texture

Let's say you have narrowed down to two diamonds, both of them are round in shape. They appear very similar to the eye. A good jeweler will have you examine the cut of the jewel. Does it have many facets, or only a few? While magnification may be necessary to see these differences, the cut of a diamond, or the texture, can have a dramatic impact on its look and shine.

It can be odd to think about texture as a visual element at first. It is more natural to think of texture as something you touch, smooth or rough, sharp or blunt, wet or dry. However, if you think about it, you can usually get the idea of how a texture will feel without having to touch it. You don't need to run your hand across gravel to determine that it will have a bumpy and rough texture (Fig. 3.8).

Alignment

Moving from one place to another is a big task. One of the more daunting parts about it is unpacking and reorganizing everything. If you have ever had to move, the feeling you have in the moment where all of your stuff is in big piles awaiting organization should resonate with you.

When you begin to organize your belongings by size, location, type, and other criteria, you are creating cohesion in your home. You are taking a bunch of stuff that feels disconnected and out of place and properly organizing and aligning those items.

With graphic design, alignment is critical to create a sense of cohesiveness and connectedness in a design. If you threw all of your shoes in a big pile, looking at that does not give a feeling that all of the shoes are connected to each other in a logical manner. When you line those shoes up on a rack by their purpose, such as dress, sport or casual, and then further align them by size and color, you have created a visual system that allows you to identify all of the individual elements and see how they relate to each other at a glance (Figs. 3.9 and 3.10).

That is what we want to do with our graphics; we want all of the elements in our graphics to be visually connected together in a way that creates a sense of ease for the audience when viewing the graphic. We want the alignment we create in our design to allow the viewer to examine the graphic in a methodical and clear-eyed way.

Repetition

Repetition is also used to create cohesion in a design. You have seen a document or Webpage at some point that used way too many different fonts and colors with no apparent rhyme or reason at all. This makes the document hard on the eyes and difficult to discern. It is easy to be distracted by all the colors and fonts to the point where it detracts from the actual writing in the document itself.

Figure 3.8 I bet with a little imagination you can feel the different textures pictured here. Visual representations of texture can create a sensation for the viewer without actually having to feel them; think of the difference when you imagine wearing a rough hewn hemp sweater compared to a billowing silk blouse.

Figure 3.9 People like to feel uncomfortable at a safe distance. That is why we have shows about hoarders, allowing us to feel the discomfort through the safety of the television screen. For many, the sight of a hoarder home before can create a feeling of anxiety, whereas the after photos give a sense of relief.

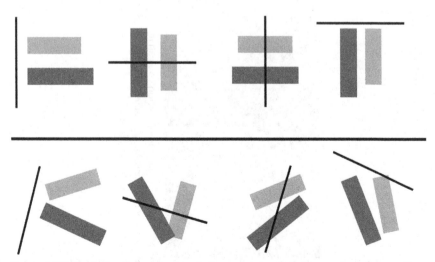

Figure 3.10 The following examples of alignment speak for themselves. Proper alignment allows for the viewer to focus on the actual material, substance, and purpose of an educational graphic and not wonky design.

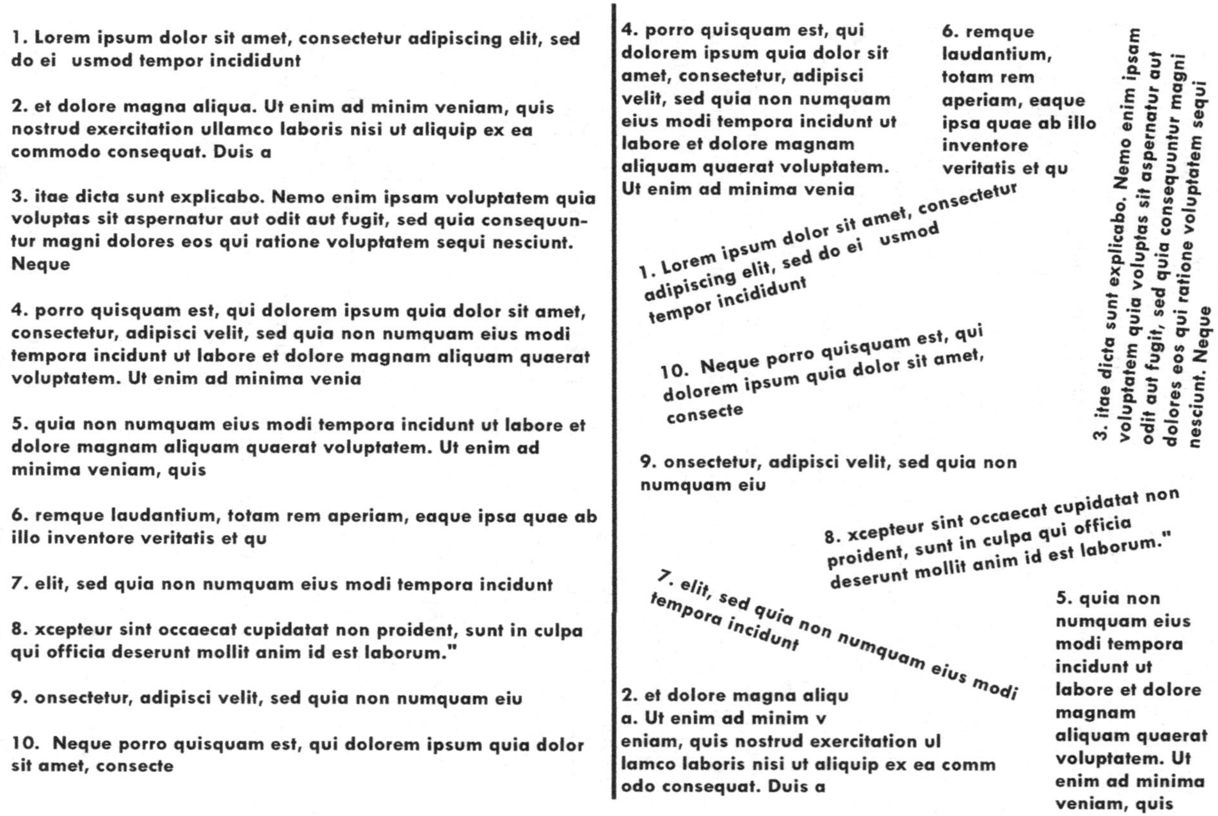

1. Lorem ipsum dolor sit amet, consectetur adipiscing elit, sed do ei usmod tempor incididunt

2. et dolore magna aliqua. Ut enim ad minim veniam, quis nostrud exercitation ullamco laboris nisi ut aliquip ex ea commodo consequat. Duis a

3. itae dicta sunt explicabo. Nemo enim ipsam voluptatem quia voluptas sit aspernatur aut odit aut fugit, sed quia consequun-tur magni dolores eos qui ratione voluptatem sequi nesciunt. Neque

4. porro quisquam est, qui dolorem ipsum quia dolor sit amet, consectetur, adipisci velit, sed quia non numquam eius modi tempora incidunt ut labore et dolore magnam aliquam quaerat voluptatem. Ut enim ad minima venia

5. quia non numquam eius modi tempora incidunt ut labore et dolore magnam aliquam quaerat voluptatem. Ut enim ad minima veniam, quis

6. remque laudantium, totam rem aperiam, eaque ipsa quae ab illo inventore veritatis et qu

7. elit, sed quia non numquam eius modi tempora incidunt

8. xcepteur sint occaecat cupidatat non proident, sunt in culpa qui officia deserunt mollit anim id est laborum."

9. onsectetur, adipisci velit, sed quia non numquam eiu

10. Neque porro quisquam est, qui dolorem ipsum quia dolor sit amet, consecte

---

4. porro quisquam est, qui dolorem ipsum quia dolor sit amet, consectetur, adipisci velit, sed quia non numquam eius modi tempora incidunt ut labore et dolore magnam aliquam quaerat voluptatem. Ut enim ad minima venia

6. remque laudantium, totam rem aperiam, eaque ipsa quae ab illo inventore veritatis et qu

1. Lorem ipsum dolor sit amet, consectetur adipiscing elit, sed do ei usmod tempor incididunt

10. Neque porro quisquam est, qui dolorem ipsum quia dolor sit amet, consecte

9. onsectetur, adipisci velit, sed quia non numquam eiu

8. xcepteur sint occaecat cupidatat non proident, sunt in culpa qui officia deserunt mollit anim id est laborum."

7. elit, sed quia non numquam eius modi tempora incidunt

2. et dolore magna aliqu a. Ut enim ad minim v eniam, quis nostrud exercitation ul lamco laboris nisi ut aliquip ex ea comm odo consequat. Duis a

5. quia non numquam eius modi tempora incidunt ut labore et dolore magnam aliquam quaerat voluptatem. Ut enim ad minima veniam, quis

3. itae dicta sunt explicabo. Nemo enim ipsam voluptatem quia voluptas sit aspernatur aut odit aut fugit, sed quia consequuntur magni dolores eos qui ratione voluptatem sequi nesciunt. Neque

Figure 3.11 The proximity of items 1 through 10 of the leftmost image make it easy on the viewer to discern what to do because 1 through 10 are in an ordered proximity to one another, while the image on the right has the opposite effect.

As you read through this book, you will notice that every element, be it the headings, sidebars, illustration comments, or bodies of text use specific fonts and are specific sizes. You will also notice that these fonts and sizes are repeated throughout from the first page to the last. This is not by accident, the layout of this book uses repetition in the typography to create a discernible pattern to establish cohesion and consistency throughout the book. This aids the reader in getting to the heart of the matter, the writing itself, without being distracted by the delivery mechanism, i.e., the book.

Proximity

Proximity is the nearness in time, space, or relationships of objects or persons. In graphic design, proximity is used to create visual unity in an illustration. For example, when you are taking notes and you create a numbered list, I bet your numbers are sequential and in an orderly row; it is easy to determine what comes first and where to read from there.

If you instead created a numbered list of items, but with each new entry randomly placed it on the page, the numbers would not longer be in a sequential or orderly list. This would mean that the sequential relationship of the numbers from smallest to largest is difficult to discern at a glance due to the poor use of proximity.

A good use of proximity will minimize or eliminate visual clutter, emphasize organization, and aid the viewer in easily comprehending the graphic (Fig. 3.11).

Good Design Disappears

One of the hallmarks of excellent design when creating graphics to convey information is that the design elements themselves disappear. If the individual elements go unnoticed, that means the designer almost assuredly did their job, and did it well. If you look at a graphic and notice that various elements don't line up correctly, or that there are too many fonts or colors, then the designer has made you notice the poor design first, and the information the graphic is intended to portray second.

SUMMARY

In this chapter we learned about the basic principles of graphic design. We learned how contrast, alignment, repetition, and proximity all play a part when creating graphics, and how these fundamentals play a role in maximizing the usefulness of our graphics for their intended purpose of educating our audience instead of design for designer's sake.

CHAPTER FOUR

Slide Design: Best Practices

Contents

Abstract

The slides in your presentation will set the tone of your presentation. Investing the time in making quality, simple, and precise slides will help ensure your effectiveness in teaching the jury about your evidence. This chapter will help you determine which information you should keep and which information you should toss when preparing your slides for court room presentation.

Keywords: Court room presentation; Effective slide; Presentations; Slide design; Technical evidence.

Information in this chapter:

- The importance of planning your slides and slide deck
- The value of simplicity
- Leveraging the power of visuals
- Creating a consistent look and feel
- Creating proper charts and graphs
- Using color and fonts effectively

Digital Forensics Trial Graphics
ISBN 978-0-12-803483-5
http://dx.doi.org/10.1016/B978-0-12-803483-5.00004-9

INTRODUCTION

The slides you use to support your testimony matter, and matter in a huge way. The slides can confuse, distract or frustrate the jury, or they can pave the way to comprehension and retention. Done well, they can be a real asset. Done poorly, they will only make your tough job even more difficult. The good news is that you can learn to create slides that truly help the jury understand and retain the key parts of your testimony. This chapter will take you through the key principles of slide design.

COMMIT THE TIME TO PLANNING AND PREPARING YOUR SLIDES AND SLIDE DECK

As you've no doubt heard, "Failing to plan is planning to fail." That old axiom holds very true for slide design. When developing a slide deck, many people mistakenly dive right in and begin building their presentation in the software of their choice. It's much better to slow down, take an "old school" approach, and start the process using pencil and paper. Instead of the computer, start with outlines, storyboards, notecards, white board, or Post-it notes (Reynolds, Prepare: Garr Reynolds, n.d.).

Start the planning process by answering this question: When you leave the witness stand, what do you want the jury to understand and ultimately remember? To answer those questions accurately and fully, you will need to consult with the attorney(s) you are working with and identify the following:
• Scope of testimony
• Key pieces of evidence and artifacts
• Technical concepts that need to be explained

As you make that determination, keep in mind that the jury will quite likely only be able to understand and retain the fundamentals of any technical explanations you make. That's no slight to the men and women of the jury, that's just being realistic. Going much beyond the basics will be a risk.

People all too often see design as being concerned entirely with how something looks.

It's not. Good design goes far beyond decoration. Sure, aesthetics plays a role, but good design is about so much more. Good design includes the following:
• Accounts for the jury's strengths and weaknesses
• Helps the jury overcome the challenges they are facing understanding and retaining your testimony

- Brings clarity
- Is the result of hard work, hard choices, deep thoughts, and lots of revision

The design addresses not only how your slide deck looks, but more importantly how it helps the jury understand the information you're presenting.

Good design can also help establish your credibility with the jury. People make instant judgments about the design of your slides, which impacts your credibility as an expert (Lidwell, 2010).

PRACTICE SIMPLICITY

Arguably, simplicity could be the most important principle of good slide design. Simplicity is essential for a couple of critical reasons. First, simplicity helps bring clarity to your slides and testimony (Reynolds, Design: Garr Reynolds, n.d.). Simplifying your slides and technical explanations makes the evidence accessible. In contrast, slides and testimony that's overly complex won't be understood and will either be ignored or even misinterpreted. Second, simplicity ensures that the slides and your testimony aren't actually creating a barrier between the jury and the evidence.

Keep in mind that simplicity isn't simple or easy to achieve. It requires hard work, empathy for the jury and the challenges they face, attention to detail, and a willingness to make hard choices.

It's important to understand what simplicity is and is not. Simplicity isn't "dumbing down" the content of your testimony. It's merely making the content accessible to the men and women on the jury.

Restraint is absolutely critical to achieve simplicity in your slides and explanations. The old saying that "less is more" couldn't ring more true in this context. Restraint separates professionals from amateurs. Adding text and graphics is easy, it's making the hard choices to cut or exclude information that often proves the most challenging. As each slide is built, you should exclude or eliminate every nonessential element (text, graphic, or animation) that you can. If you can't articulate how it helps the jury understand or retain your testimony, get rid of it. At all times, the slides should help the jury, never get in their way. Cutting is a critical part of the development process. You should cut concepts and details that don't serve a legitimate purpose. You should cut slides that don't add real value for the jury, helping them do the hard work they've been asked to do. Words and graphics should also be mercilessly cut until just the essential remains.

"Busy" or cluttered slides only obscure the real meaning of your testimony, often distracting and or frustrating the jury.

Sometimes it's hard to resist the doubt that creeps in as a result of cutting. It's a natural tendency for an expert to want to be extremely thorough, including as much as detail as possible. The problem is that too much detail and nuance can quickly overwhelm most jurors.

Unlike the old tried and true expression of "less is more," many people mistakenly do see less as "less." This can manifest itself in not just the slide design but in the content itself. In regard to the content, the amount of material covered continues to swell resulting in an overwhelmed jury.

From a design perspective, it comes down to the use of whitespace and the amount of text and visual elements on each slide. Some people are uncomfortable when large portions of the slide aren't filled with text or graphics. They may see unused space as a missed opportunity to cover more material. Good design recognizes the value of whitespace and uses it appropriately on each and every slide. Whitespace is our ally as we use our slides to teach the jury. Whitespace lets the other elements "breathe" and gives them the room they need to really communicate with the jury.

Slides that are fully crammed actually hurt you rather than help it. Complex slides, those with lots of texts and images, can overwhelm the jurors. They will have a very difficult time trying to decipher the slide and listen to your testimony. Their comprehension will definitely suffer.

Carefully consider every word and graphical element on each slide. Is the slide effective without it? If so, get rid of it. Fig. 4.1 clearly shows just how bad it can get. This slide was actually included in a briefing delivered to Gen. Stanley McChrystal in the summer of 2009. The slide was intended to convey the complexity of the American military strategy in war in Afghanistan. Mission accomplished.

"When we understand that slide, we'll have won the war," General McChrystal dryly remarked, one of his advisers recalled, as the room erupted in laughter.

Bumiller (2010).

Imagine trying to listen to the speaker while trying to sort out what this slide is trying to convey. A tall order indeed. The amount of visual "noise" in this slide is deafening.

Simplicity ensures your slides have a high signal to noise ratio. This ratio compares the relevant elements and information to those that are irrelevant. A low signal-to-noise ratio results in the degradation of the message (Reynolds, 2007).

Cut all the text you can, then cut some more. Cut the amount of text on each slide to the absolute minimum. Despite what many people think,

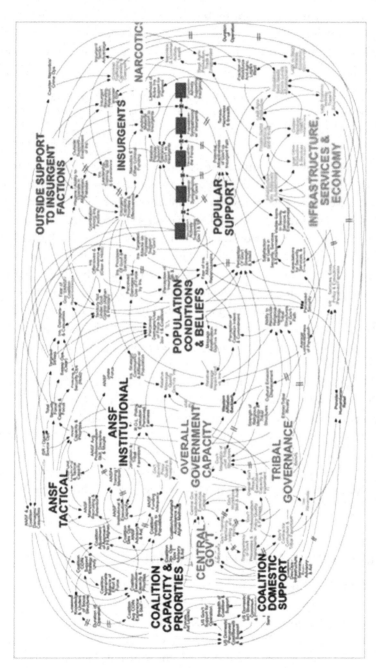

Figure 4.1 A vivid example of complexity in a slide (Bumiller, 2010).

your slides don't need complete sentences. The words on the slides support and reinforce your narration, not replace it.

Dr. John Medina, a developmental molecular biologist and author of *Brain Rules*, had this to say about how inefficient text is in a PowerPoint presentation:

> *Professionals everywhere need to know about the incredible inefficiency of text-based information and the incredible effects of images. Burn your current PowerPoint presentations and make new ones*
>
> **Medina (n.d.).**

A slide deck is not a document, at least not one in the traditional sense. As such, the rules of grammar don't apply. Cutting text can be tough. It feels counterintuitive because it destroys the complete sentences we're accustomed to writing. To many, the text-filled slides serve as a security blanket and script. They become too dependent on the slides. This dependency can be broken through time and effort spent planning, preparing, and practicing your presentation. At most, the slides should act as a hint or prompt. They should never be used as a teleprompter, with the content being read word for word.

Bullet points are terribly boring and should be avoided if at all possible. If you do decide to use bullets, use them sparingly. The best use of bullets is often as a summary of the key points at the end of the section or the presentation itself.

Modern presentation software includes a wide array of animation options. Every element on the slide can "come alive" in a seemingly limitless number of ways. Your text and images can "fly," "swivel," "zoom," "bounce," and "boomerang" into view. Just because you can, certainly doesn't mean you should. If you decide to use animation, do so sparingly. To keep things consistent, limit the number of different types of animation. Pick one and stay with it. Avoid extreme animations and keep things subtle. Choose "fades" or dissolves over "boomerangs" and "bounces."

LEVERAGE THE POWER OF VISUALS

The picture superiority effect tells us that we should use images to "improve the recognition and recall of key information" (Lidwell, 2010). Use only high-quality graphics on each slide. Avoid using "cheesy" clip art and other cartoonish images (Reynolds, Design: Garr Reynolds, n.d.). You can take your own photos and screenshots or you can buy high-quality stock photos. Don't try to stretch the images to fit the slide. Common graphic and image formats (such as .jpg, .png, and .gif) are classified as raster graphics.

Raster images are pixel based and don't resize well. When you try to resize a raster image by grabbing the side and stretching it, it becomes distorted.

Your slides will be most effective when the words and images work together. They should complement one another and support the same message or point. This sounds easy in theory but can be difficult to execute well, primarily because different people can interpret the same thing in different ways.

Use a Consistent Look and Feel

Your slide deck should have a consistent visual look and feel (i.e., theme) (Reynolds, Design: Garr Reynolds, n.d.). This visual theme consists of the fonts, background, colors, and layout. The presentation software you use likely comes with a large assortment of themes to choose from. While these default themes do provide the desired consistency, they also do little to help engage the jurors. The problem is that these templates are used over and over, to the point that the odds are that everyone has seen them. Using the "same old, same old" slide templates certainly isn't going to help you keep the jury engaged.

So, what can you do? You can create your own from scratch or you can purchase professionally developed templates.

USE THE RIGHT CHART

When done properly, charts and graphs can provide a very effective means to communicate data.

Essentially, there are basically four types of charts and graphs used in presentations: pie charts, vertical bar graphs, horizontal bar graphs, and line charts. Pie charts are excellent for showing percentages. Vertical bar charts illustrate change in quantity over time. If you want to compare quantities, a horizontal bar chart is an effective choice. Lastly, a line chart is effective at showing trends.

A major trap to avoid when building a chart or graph is trying to convey too much detail or information. Charts and graphs loaded down with details can become almost unintelligible, essentially negating their value.

USE COLOR APPROPRIATELY

Color is another important element of good design. Color can improve engagement as well as evoke emotion. Learning to use color well can significantly improve your slide deck. Colors can be grouped into two broad categories: warm and cool. Warm colors are red, yellow, orange, or

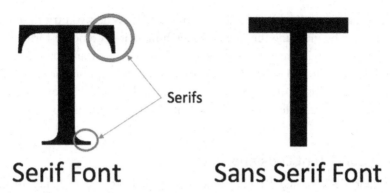

Serif Font   Sans Serif Font

Figure 4.2 Comparing a serif to a sans serif font. Note the serifs on the letter on the left.

some combination of those three. In contrast, cool colors are blue, green, purple, or some of those combined.

While we're on the topic of color, it's a good point to mention backgrounds. The color you choose for your background is very important. It can have a huge impact on the legibility of your slides. In short, there needs to be a sufficient amount of contrast between the background and the elements you place on top of it. In venues with low light, it's best to use a slide deck with a dark background. In courtrooms with better lighting, use a white background.

LIMIT THE NUMBER OF FONTS

You shouldn't use more than two different fonts in your slide deck; doing so helps keep the look and feel of your slides consistent. The type of fonts you choose can help or hurt the legibility of your text; therefore you must choose them wisely. Fonts can be classified as either serif or sans serif. A serif font is the small projections or flourishes at the ends of a letter. A sans serif font is one without those small projections (Fig. 4.2 and Table 4.1).

Generally, san serif fonts are the better choice for presentations. The reason being, the serifs can actually vanish because of the comparatively low resolution of most projectors. This is particularly true for those seated farthest away from the screen.

CONCLUSION

Fortunately, good slide design is a skill that can be learned. Good slide design starts with planning. Don't fall into the trap of diving directly into the presentation software and building your slide deck "on the fly."

Table 4.1 List of Several Common Serif and Sans Serif Fonts

Serif Fonts	Sans Serif Fonts
Bookman Old Style	Arial
Garamond	**Arial Black**
Georgia	Comic Sans MS
Lucida Bright	Helvetica
Palatino	Lucida Sans
Times New Roman	Tahoma
	Trebuchet MS
	Verdana

You should start by identifying the scope of testimony, the key pieces of evidence and artifacts, and the technical concepts that need to be explained.

Every effort should be made to simplify your slides and your testimony. This objective should never be the "dumbing down" of your presentation. The goal is and always should be to make your technical evidence accessible to the trier of fact, be it a judge or jury.

Visuals are an extremely powerful weapon in our arsenal that we can use to educate the jury. Research tells us that visuals increase recognition and recall.

Your slide deck should have a consistent look and feel from the first slide to the last. The consistent look and feel includes such elements as colors, fonts, layout, and animation.

Charts and graphs can be a fantastic way to convey and compare data. However, to actually leverage their power, it's critical to use the right chart or graph for the data in question. One chart or graph does not fit all types of data or comparisons.

The choice of colors and fonts can either help or hurt the effectiveness of your slides. They can either positively or negatively impact the legibility of the text, particularly for those at a distance.

REFERENCES

Bumiller, E. (April 26, 2010). *We have met the enemy and he is PowerPoint*. Retrieved from: http://www.nytimes.com/2010/04/27/world/27powerpoint.html?_r=0.

Lidwell, W. H. (2010). *Universal principles of design, revised and updated: 125 ways to enhance usability, influence perception, increase appeal, make better design decisions, and teach through design*. Beverly, MA: Rockport Publishers.

Reynolds, G. (March 12, 2007). *Signal-to-noise ratio and the elimination of the nonessential*. Retrieved from: http://www.presentationzen.com/presentationzen/2007/03/signaltonoise_r.html.

Reynolds, G. (n.d.). Design: Garr Reynolds. Retrieved from: http://www.garrreynolds.com/preso-tips/design/.

Reynolds, G. (n.d.). Prepare: Garr Reynolds. Retrieved from: http://www.garrreynolds.com/preso-tips/prepare/.

Presenting for Comprehension

Contents

Abstract

As an expert witness your main job in court is to teach the jury about very technical evidence. In the best of circumstance, the jury will only comprehend and remember a small portion of the information you present to them so it's your job to break down complex information into easily understandable information they can learn and remember. How you present the information will go a long way in helping you do your job effectively.

Keywords: Courtroom testimony; Expert witness; Juries; Presenting for comprehension; Teaching juries.

Information in this chapter:

- How learning works
- The characteristics of the jury as our target audience
- The courtroom versus the classroom as a learning environment
- The role of expert witness as teacher
- How to develop effective explanations
- The "curse of knowledge" and how it can impede the jury
- The expert witness as a filter

Digital Forensics Trial Graphics
ISBN 978-0-12-803483-5
http://dx.doi.org/10.1016/B978-0-12-803483-5.00005-0

INTRODUCTION

When an expert witness enters a courtroom to testify, the stakes are high and the challenges are many. Freedom, large sums of money, or even a life itself could hang in the balance. Our society relies on the justice system to protect its citizens, right wrongs, punish the guilty, and protect the innocent. At its core, the justice system in turn, depends heavily on the common sense of a select group of ordinary people to render a fair and just verdict, the jury. Many times, a jury will reach a verdict by relying primarily (or in-part) on scientific or technical evidence. In reaching a verdict, the jury will often rely on (sometimes heavily) scientific or technical evidence that they didn't understand before the trial.

Optimistically, even the most attentive and focused juror is likely to only understand a relatively small percentage of your testimony. The onus then is on you to do all that you can to give the jurors the best chance to really understand your evidence and recall it once deliberations begin.

It's important to get a full understanding of the role and responsibilities of an expert witness. Some are obvious, some not. In the legal context, you're there to share your expertise, render your opinions, and tell the truth. Your responsibility, however, goes beyond your legal and ethical requirements. You need to do as much of the hard work for jury as you can, simplifying your testimony as much as possible. If you do this, you'll give them the best chance to comprehend and retain the technical evidence you present. This is of course, easier said than done and requires very careful thought and planning well in advance of taking a seat in the witness stand.

When testifying, an expert witness essentially takes on the role of a teacher. Good teachers take their students on a journey, to a new place of understanding.

You need to see your presentation as more than words and a deck of PowerPoint slides. You need to see it as a critical tool used to facilitate jury learning and understanding. It's a key part in the legal process, intentionally designed to enhance jury understanding and retention.

In keeping with the journey analogy, you could also see your role as that of a guide. Good guides ensure that no one is left behind no matter how long or how difficult the trip. If you are to succeed in getting everyone to the destination, much thought and effort must be invested into the planning process. Revision and editing are key elements of this process. During the early stage of development, you need to expose your work to others, preferably lay people, to collect valuable feedback. This feedback is intended to give you a solid sense of how understandable your slides and testimony are and catch all the jargon and acronyms you may be oblivious to.

HOW LEARNING WORKS

Learning is often thought of as an abstract, intangible process. In reality, it's really not. It's actually quite physical. Scientific research has shown us that when learning occurs, it causes an actual physical change in the brain. The goal of your testimony is to increase the knowledge of the jurors, so ultimately what you're really trying to do is create a physical change in their brain. Having a fundamental understanding of some basic brain anatomy as well as what you can do to cause those changes will help you become more effective from the witness seat.

Gaining a fundamental understanding of how people learn will help us craft your testimony and visuals in a way that truly helps the jury reach a new level of understanding. This will afford the jury the best chance of understanding and using the information you give them.

Research by cognitive psychologists has also shown us that our knowledge, our expertise, and our memories are organized into webs. These webs, also known as neuronal networks, exist for everything we know (Zull, 2002). This prior knowledge is a physical, tangible thing. Fig. 5.1 provides a simple visual example of a neuronal network.

The stronger a connection is, the easier that information is to recall. In a classroom environment, effective teachers employ a wide range of strategies designed

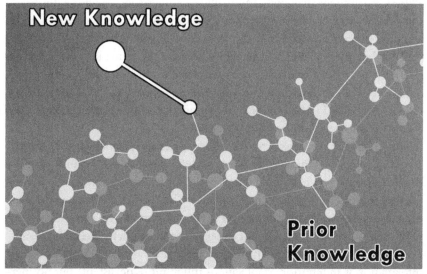

Figure 5.1 A simple neuronal network depicting prior knowledge. It's always best to connect new knowledge or concepts to existing knowledge to improve understanding and retention. Using an appropriate analogy is one way to do that.

to build and strengthen these connections. One of the most effective approaches students and teachers use to learn is called retrieval practice. Practice quizzes and flash cards are two common examples of retrieval practice. The daunting challenge for the expert witness in the courtroom is that many of the most effective teaching tools aren't available to you, effectively tying your hands behind your back.

This is the scientific reasoning behind using analogies and examples that are familiar to the jurors. Ideally, any new information that you introduce can find somewhere in the juror's existing neuronal network to connect. David Ausubel, a noted educational psychologist, put the importance of connecting to prior knowledge this way: "The single most important factor influencing learning is what the learner already knows. Ascertain this and teach him accordingly" (Ausubel, 1968). Every juror we speak to comes to the jury box with prior knowledge that will impact how they process our explanations. Ignoring this will impact our effectiveness (Zull, 2002).

When creating examples as part of your explanations and exhibits, you need to seek applicable common ground with juror's existing knowledge and experiences. The prior knowledge that jurors bring can serve as an anchor for the new knowledge you hope to convey (Ambrose, 2010). Just like a Velcro wall, it gives it a place to "stick." So, what does that look like? Let's say, for example, you need the jury to understand IP addresses. What thing or experience has the jury had that is most analogous to an IP address? A street address is definitely analogous and would be understood by all the jurors.

On the surface, a juror with a lot (or even some) prior knowledge of the technical aspects of your testimony may seem like an advantage. It may very well be, but there are exceptions. Just because the prior knowledge exists doesn't mean that it's correct or even complete. In this instance the previously existing neuronal network may become more of a hindrance than a helper (Ambrose, 2010). For example, erroneous prior knowledge can cause a juror to misunderstand expert testimony.

In general terms, people have two types of memory; working and long term. Working memory functions in some respects just like the volatile memory (RAM) in a computer. Working memory holds the information we're currently focused or working on. The working memory, like RAM, is volatile in the sense that it's fragile and disappears easily. People can typically hold about three to four things in working memory at any given time (Gathercole, 2007).

In contrast, long-term memory functions such as a hard drive where the information is much more stable and is much more persistent (but not permanent). Working memory does have limitations making the information held there vulnerable in a few different ways. We can lose data in working

Table 5.1 Threats to Juror Working Memory Along With Strategies Experts Can Use to Mitigate Them

Threats to Working Memory	Mitigation Strategy
Distraction—typically an interruption of some kind or a random thought popping in our head.	Keep the jury engaged, use effective visuals, use stories, use concrete examples.
Exceeding capacity—like a PC, our brains have a finite amount of working memory.	Filter for the jury giving them just the information they need, resist getting too detailed, use progressive disclosure ("builds") in your slides.
Difficult mental task—when we are working on something complicated.	Simplify your verbal testimony and your slides. Eliminate or fully explain jargon and acronyms in terms accessible to the jury.

memory if we become distracted, try to take in too much information at one time, or by processing a difficult task (Gathercole, 2007).

• Distraction—typically an interruption of some kind or a random thought popping in our head.
• Exceeding capacity—like a PC, our brains have a finite amount of working memory. When we exceed our capacity, information in working memory is lost. For example, most of us have no problem multiplying 5 times 5. However, the resources needed to calculate 397 times 681 will likely exceed the working memory of most people (Gathercole, 2007).
• Difficult mental task—when we are working on something complicated, the memory resources needed to process that task can push out information that was already in working memory.

As you work through your explanations you need to keep in mind these limitations and do all that you cannot to distract, overwhelm, or overwork the juror's working memory. Table 5.1 outlines some common threats to your working memory and what we can do to mitigate the threat.

Our working memory is closely connected to what we are currently focused on. We need to maintain focus on a subject to keep it in our working memory.

As if there weren't enough threats to a juror's working memory, stress can also take a serious toll (Weinschenk, 2012). Just being a juror can be stressful to some. Jury duty can require jurors to miss significant time away from both work and their families. This can cause both emotional and financial hardship in addition to the added frustration of falling behind at work. Jurors can also feel the weight of rendering a verdict in a case that could have major consequences for the parties involved.

This means that some jurors could be stressed out before an expert witness has uttered a word.

In one study, jurors from four separate criminal trials were interviewed. In two of the cases, the defendants were on trial for murder. In the remaining two cases, one defendant was on trial for child abuse and the other for obscenity-related charges. In total, the authors spoke with 40 individual jurors. Of the 40, 27 reported one (or more) physical symptoms. These symptoms included the following:

- gastrointestinal distress (10 jurors)
- generalized nervousness (4 jurors)
- heart palpitation (6 jurors)
- headaches (4 jurors)
- sexual inhibitions (4 jurors)
- depression (4 jurors)
- anorexia (4 jurors)
- faintness (2 jurors)
- numbness, lump in throat, chest pain, hives, and flu (1 juror each)
  Kaplan (1992)

It's relatively easy to overload working memory, especially with expert testimony on a highly technical subject.

TARGET AUDIENCE: THE JUDGE AND JURY

In many respects the jury represents a wildcard in the legal process. The attorneys do their best, within the confines of the system, to empanel a jury that will most likely deliver the verdict for their client. But there is only so much they can do.

Being a juror is hard, very hard. The responsibility is great with lives literally hanging in the balance in some instances. Our system of justice hinges on average citizens serving as finders of fact in civil and criminal matters. The verdicts rendered by juries often rely (sometimes heavily) on scientific or highly technical evidence.

You've had years of training and experience to learn your craft. Compare that to the technology training and experience of the average juror. In all likelihood, there really is no comparison. The odds are excellent that the majority of jurors are learning about much of this information for the first time.

As experts charged with imparting your expertise to the men and women of the jury, you need to understand who the people are sitting in that jury box. This is absolutely critical because they're the most important people in the courtroom. Jury pools are typically diverse in regard to their age, sex, race, education, occupations, experiences, etc. They come to jury duty with different backgrounds, capacities, and beliefs that can help or hinder their ability to understand, evaluate, and apply the technical testimony they hear. This understanding should guide you as you both prepare and deliver your testimony. Ignoring this reality would be a mistake and can have a negative impact your effectiveness (Smith, 2002).

Jurors face significant challenges in the execution of their duties. One minute they are feeling the tremendous burden of their responsibilities, while in the next minute they are bored out of their minds. They are forced to take time away from their work, family, and friends. All of this is in addition to the potential feelings of confusion and frustration brought about by overly complex and poorly delivered expert testimony. In this context, it's easy to see the potential to raise a juror's stress level.

If you think about it, the courtroom is not an ideal learning environment. Although understanding is the objective in both, courtrooms certainly aren't classrooms (Meyer, 1998). They differ in many significant ways including the layout, the way information is delivered, and the roles and responsibilities of participants just to name a few. These differences will work against you as you try to teach the jurors.

Jurors come from all walks of life. They come with a variety of levels of education, experiences, attitudes toward technology, and attitudes toward their jury service. Each juror also brings with them different abilities to learn and retain information. They also bring with them other filters through which your testimony must pass including worldview, experiences, biases, etc.

Let's use some numbers to paint a rough picture of the educational level of our potential jury pool. Table 5.2 compares some of the common data points between the most recent census (2015) and an article published by Cornell Law Faculty Publications (Kaye, Hans, Dann, Farley, & Albertson, 2007).

Table 5.2 Some Statistics We Can Use to Gain Some General Sense of the Educational Level of the Jury

2015 US Census	Cornell Law Faculty Article
Nine out of ten adults (88%) had at least a GED or high school diploma.	49% had at least a GED or high school diploma
One in three (33%) had a BA	N/A
The percentage of men (32%) and women (33%) with a BA was nearly the same	N/A
59% of adults finished some college credits	33% had some college
12% had advanced degrees (MAs or PhDs)	12% had postgraduate degree
Ryan (2016)	Kaye et al. (2007)

Furthermore, the findings in the Cornell Law Faculty article indicate that the following:

- 5% of jury pool has less than high school diploma
- Most jurors reported taking some science and/or math classes in high school (average 4 classes)
- 43% reported having job related science/math experience
  Kaye et al. (2007)

One might suspect that younger members of the perspective jury pool would have a command of fundamental technology skills given that they have essentially grown up "digital." There are some statistics however, that cast some serious doubt on that suspicion. According to a report by Change the Equation, millennials (those born between 1982 and 1994) spend an average "35 h per week on digital media," 58% of them "have low skills in solving problems with technology" (Change the Equation, 2015).

Not all jurors think the same way. Some are more analytical thinkers, deliberately evaluating your testimony and the evidence. Other jurors are more emotional, placing more value on a witness' likeability rather than the evidence they present.

Jurors are just like the rest of us, they don't want to be bored. One sure-fire way to bore a jury is to stand there and read slides loaded with paragraphs of text or bullet after bullet. The first thing we can do to increase juror engagement is to swear off the aforementioned presentation methods that have likely put us to sleep at one time or another. Next, we need to use quality, appropriate visuals as much as we can. Stories are another powerful way to keep jurors engaged and focused.

Attention span is another obstacle for jurors. One study done by Microsoft shows the average adult attention span dropping from 12 s in 2000 to 8 s in 2013. That is, according to the study, 1 s less than a typical gold fish (Microsoft Canada, 2015).

Not surprisingly, stress has a negative impact on the learning process. You can unintentionally add to juror stress if your testimony confuses rather than teaches them.

THE LEARNING ENVIRONMENT: COURTROOM VERSUS CLASSROOM

One significant obstacle in your path as expert witnesses turned teacher is the setting you'll be working in. As a learning environment, the courtroom is a far cry from the classroom. It is definitely less than ideal for

Table 5.3 Comparing the Learning Environment of the Classroom and the Courtroom

Classroom	Courtroom
Teacher evaluates students	Jurors evaluate experts
Outcome impacts student	Outcome impacts third party (victim, defendant, society, etc.).
Teacher controls presentation	Third party (attorney) controls presentation
Students participate	Jurors observe
Teacher can reinforce lecture with active learning exercises	Essentially "lecture" only
Can use visuals	Can use visuals
Students can ask questions	Jurors can't ask questions
Students can read/study beforehand	Jurors can't read/study beforehand
Teacher can assess student's progress and adjust/address	Expert can't assess juror's learning/ understanding

what we need to accomplish (Meyer, 1998). Many of the tried and true classroom strategies that enable or reinforce learning simply aren't available to you in the courtroom. These practices include homework, the ability to ask questions, practice exercises, tests, discussions, and quizzes just to name a few. You need to recognize the existence of these hurdles and get over, around, or through them by taking advantage of all the other opportunities you do have. Table 5.3 compares and contrasts the courtroom and the classroom as a learning environment.

If a jury understands anything, it will be the basics (Smith, 2002). Teaching the basics can have the added benefit of helping you build a rapport with the jury and establish your credibility. As we learned in Chapter 3, the visuals you use are critical. The visuals may be what a jury remembers the most. Well-prepared visuals that actually help the jury (from their perspective, not yours) show them respect. You owe it to the jury to give them tools that help them, not make their job any harder than it already is. Well-prepared visuals are one "tool" the expert witness can give them.

EXPLANATIONS

Crafting and delivering an effective explanation is no easy feat. It requires a good deal of thought, preparation, and practice. The Merriam-Webster Dictionary defines explanation as "the act or process of making something clear or easy to understand..." This sounds like language from the job description for an expert witness. It's easy to lose sight of this objective when you testify, especially during cross-examination or even redirect. Your direct testimony can be much more thought-out, planned, and controlled. Cross-examination and redirect is much less so. Those questions can come in rapid fire sequence while under stress. In these moments, under those conditions, it's easy to slip back into your "native tongue" and litter your answers with jargon and complexity.

Analogies are another powerful tool at your disposal. Analogies refer to something that's familiar or clearly understood, to explain something more difficult and harder to comprehend. Analogies are effective because they activate a juror's prior knowledge (Zull, 2002). Scientific research has shown us the critical link between learning and what an individual (Napier, 2014) already knows. Analogies can unlock this prior knowledge. There are some well-known analogies in our field. A successful expert witness invests the time to learn and develop effective analogies (Meyer, 1998). Good analogies can be used on more than one case. As such, stockpiling them is strongly encouraged. Table 5.4 lists some common analogies used in digital forensics.

The Art of Explanation by Lee LeFever provides some very helpful guidance and tools for experts in crafting explanations. LeFever's Explanation Scale gives you a visual reference you can use to plot a juror's current level of understanding as well as where you want them to be after you testify (LeFever, 2012) (Fig. 5.2).

The scale is a simple graduated continuum going from left (a state of less understanding) to the right (more understanding). See Fig. 5.3.

Keep in mind, as individuals, not all jurors will have the same starting point on the LeFever scale. Your mission as an expert witness is to move the jurors from their respective starting position to some point to the right.

Speaking generally, it's a safe bet that more jurors will start closer to "A" (Less Understanding) than the "Z" (More Understanding). While you are trying to move them down the scale to the right, it's important to know that your ultimate target isn't Z. Getting every juror to "Z" is not only unnecessary, but risky to even attempt. You don't need to make experts ("Z") out of the jury. As you know now, the courtroom is far from the ideal learning environment. Trying to convey that much complex

Table 5.4 Common Analogies Used in Digital Forensics

Term/Concept	Analogy
Hash value	Digital fingerprint/digital DNA
Hard drive	Filing cabinet
IP address	Street address
File allocation table	Card catalogue/book index

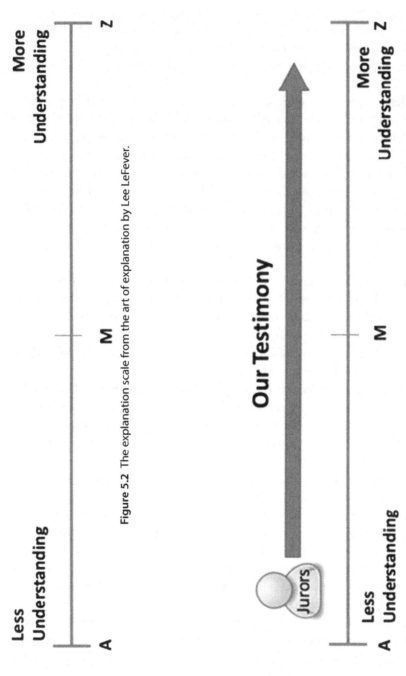

Figure 5.2 The explanation scale from the art of explanation by Lee LeFever.

Figure 5.3 The quality and effectiveness of our testimony and exhibits move the jurors down LeFever's scale to a point of more understanding.

information will likely confuse and ultimately frustrate the jurors. Not exactly the outcome you want. The odds are, if jurors are going to grasp anything from your testimony, it's going to be the fundamentals. Moving beyond the basics is not done without risk. Moving jurors a few points to the right of their starting point is both more realistic and less risky (Fig. 5.4).

Despite your best efforts, you need to accept the fact that not every juror will fully "get" what you're trying to explain. All you can do is try to maximize each and every opportunity you have to educate the jury, using proven strategies designed to foster understanding and retention.

When crafting your explanation, start with something tangible and specific, something that is familiar to the jurors. This will help anchor the new information in the juror's mind (i.e., their current neuronal network). The more you can connect with information or experiences they already have, the more likely they are to understand and retain this new information.

As in contracts, politics, and diplomacy, words matter. Actually, they matter a lot. The words you choose can have a direct impact, good or bad, on the effectiveness of your testimony. In all likelihood, you won't be able to avoid using some jargon and acronyms. However, you are always more effective delivering your testimony using everyday language as opposed to technical terms that are unfamiliar to the jury.

Using vivid language helps the jury "see" with their mind's eye what you're talking about and can assist them in retaining what you tell them. They need to connect the unfamiliar with the familiar, anchoring the new information into their existing knowledge. Once they do, they can process more complex material.

Repetition helps with retention, try to summarize each chunk or section before moving on to the next. A final review of the key points at the end of the presentation can also help bolster retention. Remember, if they don't retain it, they won't be able to use it when they deliberate. This becomes even more challenging when the deliberations occur days or even weeks after your testimony. In this situation, using these principles to maximize the jury's chances of retaining the key pieces of your testimony would be even more important.

As you roll through your testimony, you need to illustrate only one concept at a time. Again, in court, it's very easy to overwhelm jurors with highly technical explanations. One way to prevent this is by using "builds" in your slides.

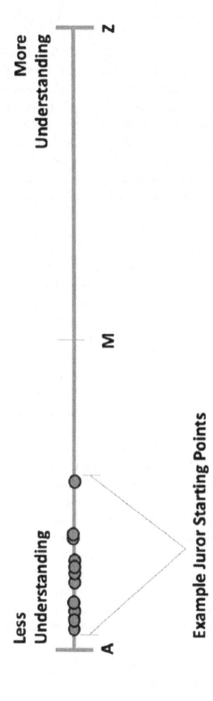

Example Juror Starting Points

Figure 5.4 Typical jurors are going to start on the left side of LeFever's scale of understanding. As you can see, it's quite a distance all the way to "Z." Even attempting to cover that much ground through expert testimony is quite risky and unrealistic.

Builds take some of the cognitive pressure off the jury by introducing (or highlighting) one element of the slide/graphic at a time, rather than all at once.

Some experts make the mistake of trying to cover too much in their explanations. They cover much more ground than necessary given the question asked or the facts of the case. Trial testimony shouldn't necessarily sound like a college lecture. Keep a close eye on the content and cut down material to the minimum they need to know to understand the evidence. Many times this is done out of an abundance of caution by an expert to be thorough and precise. Keep in mind, the jury doesn't need to know everything you know about the subject in question. More often than not, they just need to understand the basics. The more you add, the bigger the burden you place on the jury and the more likely you are to overwhelm or confuse them.

You should be merciless in cutting down the content (Duarte, 2010). As you develop your slides, you need to ask yourself some tough questions. Why should this information be included? Is this information the jury MUST understand to render an accurate verdict? Is this material basic or more advanced? Is the level of detail helpful or distracting? You should keep cutting until you get the minimum the jury needs to do their work.

It's the expert's responsibility to simplify this content as much as possible. When you simplify, you're removing the major obstacles in the way of jury understanding. That said, you're not "dumbing down" the content, you're just making it accessible. Referring to simplifying as "dumbing down" is disrespectful to the men and women on the jury, the most vital people in the courtroom.

We've been using the journey analogy throughout this chapter to describe your testimony. In keeping with that analogy, providing the jury with a roadmap (the major topics) of your testimony can be quite helpful to them (Meyer, 1998). It gives the jury some high-level idea of where your testimony is taking them and what to expect. This roadmap typically takes the form of a PowerPoint slide listing the topics to be covered and presented at the start of an explanation or testimony. This same slide can also be used as a "sign post," indicating where on the journey you are at any given time. This "sign post" slide could be inserted at the start of each new topic.

The structure (order) of your slide deck is critical. Done well, it can provide a solid path for the journey the jury will take. Done poorly, our journey will be fraught with pitfalls, roadblocks, and cognitive wrong turns. The "slide sorter" view in our presentation software is one of the best tools we can use to set or tweak.

EXPERT AS TEACHER

The best expert witnesses have the ability to teach effectively when they are on the stand. They take the most complex subject matter, distill it down to the basics, thereby making it accessible to as many people on the jury as possible. Teaching well is a complicated process. There are many points where the process can break down and slow or even impede learning. If you can effectively teach the jury, your evidence will have real value. If you can't, your evidence stands the very real chance of being partially or even completely ignored. If they don't understand it, what other choice does the jury have?

As teachers in the courtroom, one of your major responsibilities is to manage the cognitive load of your students (i.e., the jury) (Anderson, 2016). What is cognitive load? Cognitive load refers to the burden placed on your mind's working memory as you process information.

There are several strategies you can employ to help the jurors by reducing the cognitive load. You can reduce the cognitive load of your target audience by doing the heavy lifting in advance of your testimony. During the planning and preparation process, you should keep in mind the limitations of the jurors working memory and reduce that load when and where you can.

Traditionally speaking, humans are known to have five recognized senses; sight, hearing, taste, smell, and touch. Your testimony is essentially delivered via two primary sensory "channels," through your sense of sight or hearing. At different points, one or both channels will be in use at any given time. When you have information being delivered on both channels simultaneously, they are going to compete for processing resources in the brain. Complexity in either "channel" increases cognitive load (Anderson, 2016) (Fig. 5.5).

Picture an expert testifying in a trial. As he's or she's testifying, he's or she's standing in front of a large projection screen. Under direct examination, his/her attorney has just asked him/her to explain to the jury members what an MD5 hash value is. "MD5 stands for Message Digest Five" he begins, "and is a type hashing algorithm. MD5 outputs a 128-bit, hexadecimal number..." As he/she testifies, on the screen behind him/her is a slide with three individual paragraphs of text separated as bullet points. The slide contains nothing but text and is devoid of any visual elements.

In this situation jurors are put at a significant cognitive disadvantage, trying to take in what the expert is saying at the same time they are reading

Figure 5.5 It's relatively easy to create a cognitive overload during expert testimony. Too much complexity in either the auditory or visual channels can create this situation.

the slide. They may be hearing you, but are they really listening? Those two things aren't the same, and they certainly aren't equal in terms of comprehension. To reduce the cognitive load in this situation, you need to do two things; reduce the amount of text on the slide and eliminate the jargon from what you are saying.

Are humans capable of doing two (or more) things at once? A better question might be are humans capable of doing those things equally well? Research has given us the answer and that answer is clearly no (Napier, 2014). We've been conditioned over the years to believe that multitasking is both a useful and beneficial skill, well-worth cultivating and practicing. This, however, is a myth. There are certainly things we're capable of doing simultaneously that results in little to no adverse impact. Walking and chewing gum (for most of us) and driving a car while listening to the radio come to mind. Learning and understanding, however, are not in that same category. From a strictly cognitive perspective, there is a cost to be paid for multitasking (Napier, 2014).

Like images, diagrams can be extremely useful in increasing the effectiveness of your testimony. For diagrams with multiple parts, layers, or labels, using "builds" may be the most effective way to introduce the illustration along with the concepts it covers. A build simply refers to the use of the animation function in the presentation software to "build" the slide, one element at a time. This build technique could be used with graphics or text. The build method keeps the jury from being overwhelmed with a lot of information (visual or text) all at once. The build presents one element at a time, giving the jury the chance to process one piece of information at a time. When you hit them with new information all at once, you're essentially asking the jury to drink from a fire hose.

THE EXPERT WITNESS AS FILTER

In reality, the jury doesn't need to know every single thing about a particular topic and they certainly don't need to know everything you know. For a multitude reasons, you must also serve as a filter for the jury. Ideally, you need to give them enough of the technical details so they can fully understand and appreciate the evidence but no more.

When you don't filter, you force the jury to work too hard (Duarte, 2010). You can create confusion where there didn't need to be. You needlessly muddy the water. Remember, the jury is quite likely only going to understand and retain the basics. Asking them to learn and retain large amounts of technical nuance is both unwise and unreasonable. It's your responsibility to cut and keep cutting until your testimony and visuals are distilled down to their core, fundamental elements, in other words, the basics. Your cutting should be merciless. It should be broad (cutting topics, concepts, and slides) to more focused (cutting text, and images). Nothing is off-limits and nothing extraneous should survive the process. What should you look at cutting? Here's a short list:

- Topics
- Concepts
- Slides
- Text
- Images

Remember, you are filtering (i.e., cutting) for the benefit of the jury. When some people present, they use the words on the screen as a crutch, reading them in some instances word for word. This may help the presenter, but can hurt the jury from a cognitive perspective. From the expert witness perspective, the text on the slide are better thought of as a prompt rather than a script. Cutting, especially text, can be unnerving for the presenter. Most of us have been presenting using text-filled slides for many, many years. Having that text on the slide does provide some degree of comfort for the unprepared presenter. Again, you need to be mindful that the slides are there for the benefit of the audience, not the presenter.

Witnesses in nearly all instances are encouraged to keep their answers brief. Brevity has some obvious tactical advantages in a trial, but it also has some potential benefit for the jury in helping to reduce their cognitive load.

Putting these practices to use will require you to apply several constraints to both your testimony and slides. Much of what is recommended runs counter to the majority of presentations we've seen and to the way we've presented in the past. In that light, it's easy to view these limitations as a hindrance. In addition to the many benefits as already discussed, these constraints also aide in increasing the clarity of your presentation. The final presentation that comes out of this process should be leaner and more accessible to the majority of jurors.

CURSE OF KNOWLEDGE

Sometimes your testimony can suffer from a curse even more potent than one cast by Gypsy priestess. Commonly called the "curse of knowledge," it refers to the difficulty in picturing what it's like for someone else that doesn't know what you know (Anderson, 2016). This is a very real and all too common problem for expert witnesses. You talk about digital forensics, you read about digital forensics, and you write about digital forensics. It becomes a second language for you. Speaking in your "native tongue" comes natural to you and you do it all the time. In fact, you don't even realize you're doing it most of the time. On a typical day at work, surrounded by your technically astute colleagues, this isn't a problem. On the witness stand however, in front of a jury, it can become a stone-cold killer of comprehension for the jury. The testimony of an expert witness under the curse is laden with jargon and acronyms as well as unnecessary details. Technical concepts, likely foreign to most of the jurors, go unexplained. The curse is somewhat easier to control during direct examination when the testimony has been thought-out and prepared in advance. Cross-examination (and perhaps to a lesser extent redirect) offer the best opportunity for an expert to inadvertently revert back to the highly technical language they've grown accustomed to.

The good news is that there are concrete steps you can take to avoid being cursed in this manner, simple awareness being the crucial first step. Don't assume the jury knows anything about computers or other technology. Every technical term or concept should be fully explained and simplified in plain, concrete language. Bombarding the jury with terms such as "slack space," "data carving," "write blocked," and "bit-stream image" will shut them down. The odds are that you've experienced a very similar situation yourself. Think back to a time in school when a teacher launched into an explanation that was filled with jargon and material you didn't understand. How did that make you feel? Odds are at best confused and at worst frustrated and demeaned. A trip to the doctor's office could have also given you a similar experience. Unfortunately, many doctors and other medical professionals also suffer from the curse of knowledge. They often talk to their patients using medical terminology that confuses what they're trying to get across rather than clarifies.

A juror who is shut down will quickly become disengaged. A juror who is disengaged isn't going to understand our testimony let alone retain it. In other words, your evidence will be ignored. If that happens, you've failed not only your client but the juror and justice system as well.

This curse of knowledge causes you to assume (many times even subconsciously) that the jury has knowledge and understanding that they actually don't.

It's easy to forget who you're really talking to during a trial. An attorney (or perhaps the judge) asks you a question and the natural instinct is to answer it using the technical language of your profession. Before you even realize it, the jargon and acronyms come spilling out as part of your answer.

Lay colleagues, friends, and family can provide extremely valuable feedback on your slide deck and explanations (Anderson, 2016). These folks are perfect substitutes for the actual jury you'll face during trial. Like a canary in a coal mine, they can provide early warning of any unexplained jargon or other confusing material. The value of letting them conduct this sort of preview can't be over stated (Fig. 5.6).

Again, you need to put yourselves in the jury's seat. They have a very difficult task as it is. You certainly don't need to add to the difficulty by asking them to sift through your jargon looking for the information they need.

CONCLUSION

Learning causes physical changes in the brain. Some of the techniques and best practices used by teachers in the classroom to facilitate learning can also help us as expert witnesses in the courtroom. A well-crafted explanation is not easy to produce. It requires considerable thought and preparation. When delivering an explanation to the jury, analogies are a powerful tool that can be used to bolster understanding. New knowledge is more likely to be understood and retained when it can be tied to existing knowledge. As teachers in the courtroom, you need to identify relevant prior knowledge possessed by the jury and use it as an anchor point or foothold for your testimony.

It's no secret that the objective of your testimony is to move the jury from a point of less understanding to one of more understanding. An expert must keep in mind that it's unnecessary, unrealistic, and unproductive to attempt to move the jury too far down the continuum. To do so risks losing, confusing, and frustrating the jury. Technical jargon and acronyms must be fully explained or eliminated from your testimony and slides.

Being a juror is often difficult and stressful work. Having empathy for the jury will make us far more effective. As expert witnesses, you need to recognize their challenges and do everything you can to make their jobs easier, not harder. As experts, it's easy to forget what it's like not to know something. You can't assume the jury knows anything. Known as the "curse of knowledge," this problem typically manifests itself when our testimony and slides are riddled with jargon and acronyms.

The role of the expert witness during a trial goes significantly beyond the testimony that he or she provides. The best experts take on the additional

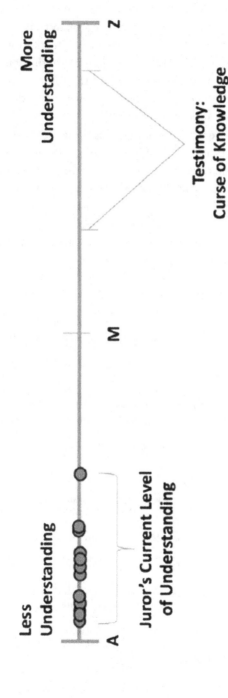

Figure 5.6 Here we see an example of where expert testimony could plot on LeFever's scale in contrast to the likely starting point of the jury. When testifying under the effects of the curse of knowledge, your answers are often too far to the right to be effective.

role of teacher, transferring basic expertise to the jury. Good teachers work hard to reduce the cognitive load on their students. What you say, how you say it, and how your slides are constructed matters. It can have a huge impact, positive or negative, on your effectiveness. In addition to serving as a teacher, you must also serve as a filter for the jury. In this sense, your job is to distill your testimony and visuals down into the minimal amount needed to get the job done. In other words, your objective is to reduce the amount of "noise" the jury both sees and hears.

While you need to embrace your role as a teacher in the courtroom, you also need to understand the many ways the courtroom differs from the classroom. Much of what occurs in a typical classroom to facilitate learning can't be done in a court of law. These differences include how information is presented; homework, readings, exercises, real-time questions, and student participation just to name a few. If we can embrace the role of teacher in the classroom, whose responsibility is to educate and facilitate jury learning, we will become far more effective on the witness stand.

REFERENCES

Ambrose, S. A. (2010). *How learning works: Seven research-based principles for smart teaching.* Hoboken, NJ: Jossey-Bass.

Anderson, C. (2016). *TED talks: The official TED guide to public speaking.* Boston: Houghton Mifflin Harcourt.

Ausubel, D. P. (1968). *Educational psychology: A cognitive view.* Toronto: Holt, Rinehart & Winston of Canada, Ltd.

Change the Equation. (2015). *Does not compute the high cost of low technology skills in the U.S.— and what we can do about it.* Washington: Change the Equation.

Duarte, N. (2010). *Resonate: Present visual stories that transform audiences.* Hoboken, NJ: John Wiley and Sons.

Gathercole, S. E. (2007). *Understaning working memory: A classroom guide.* London: Harcourt Assessment.

Kaplan, S. M. (1992). The occupational hazards of jury duty. *Journal of American Academy of Psychiatry and the Law, 20*(3), 325–333.

Kaye, D. H., Hans, V. P., Dann, B. M., Farley, E. J., & Albertson, S. (2007). *Statistics in the jury box: How jurors respond to mitochondrial DNA match probabilities.* Cornell Law Faculty Publications, 363.

LeFever, L. (2012). *The art of explanation: Making your ideas, products, and services easier to understand.* Hoboken, NJ: Wiley.

Meyer, C. (1998). *Expert witnessing: Explaining and understanding science.* Boca Raton: CRC Press.

Microsoft Canada. (2015). *Attention spans: Consumer insights.* Vancouver: Microsoft.

Napier, N. K. (May 12, 2014). *The myth of multitasking: Think you can multitask well? Think again.* Retrieved from Psychology Today: https://www.psychologytoday.com/blog/creativity-without-borders/201405/the-myth-multitasking.

Ryan, C. L. (2016). *Educational attainment in the United States: 2015. U.S. Census Bureau.* Washington: U.S. Census Bureau.

Smith, F. C. (2002). *A guide to forensic testimony: The art and practice of presenting testimony as an expert technical witness*. Boston: Addison-Wesley Professional.

Weinschenk, S. (2012). *100 things every presenter needs to know about people*. San Francisco, USA: New Riders.

Zull, J. E. (2002). *The art of changing the brain: Enriching the practice of teaching by exploring the biology of learning*. Sterling, VA, USA: Stylus Publishing.

CHAPTER SIX

Putting It All Together

Contents

Abstract

Examples of how to make simple effective visuals to explain complex technical issues are explained in this chapter, as well as a presentation from a real case.

Keywords: Compousssnd file; Court; Disk image; Expert testimony; Jury; Presentation; Technical illustration.

Information in this chapter:

- A real-case example of complicated technical issues explained in plain language
- How illustrations can be used to build on one another to aid in explaining complex technical issues

INTRODUCTION

Now that we have laid the foundation of how useful graphics can be when explaining a technical concepts to laypersons, let's see what it is like when the rubber hits the road. This chapter is an example of a couple of graphics I have used to explain technical concepts, and then we will examine a presentation I have used to explain the digital evidence in a highly complex case using plain language and graphics.

Before we go any further through a disclaimer is needed. To my technical friends, it is important to remember that a graphic is similar to an analogy in a critical way; an analogy is very useful to explain something in plain language, but if you squeeze any analogy hard enough, it breaks down.

Digital Forensics Trial Graphics
ISBN 978-0-12-803483-5
http://dx.doi.org/10.1016/B978-0-12-803483-5.00006-2

A graphic is the same. It can be used to explain something in our context at a high level, to get the main points across. If a graphic was used in an attempt to explain a technical concept on a computer system in its entirety, it would be huge, bloated, convoluted, and imminently confusing.

EXAMPLE GRAPHICS WITH EXPLANATION

Let's warm up with a couple of examples where a graphic is used to explain a single technical concept.

Explanation: How Browser Caching Works

As you surf the Internet, the Web browser you are using saves information to your computer in temporary storage. This process of saving Web pages and documents in temporary storage is called Internet browser caching or Web caching. The purpose of Web caching is to improve the experience of the computer user as he or she browses the Internet. When you visit a website, your Web browser will begin to save the information that you are viewing to your computer and also parts of a website that you are not viewing. So while you are at the home

This is all you see

But all of this is saved to your computer

page of a website, your browser might be temporarily saving the other pages also. The browser is anticipating that you will look at the other pages and images on the website, and it saves this information so that it will load faster when you navigate to them. The browser is attempting to make your experience better by downloading information you have not seen so that it loads very quickly when you navigate the website. However, information now exists on your computer that you may have never seen before.

Explanation: LNK (Link Files)

Link files are files that exist for the sole purpose of pointing to another file. For example, the icons on your desktop are Link files. Your software applications live inside of the folder Program Files, the Link files just allows you to access the program easily from the "Shortcut" (Link file) on your desktop. From your start menu, if you select "Recent Files," the listed files are also Link files, allowing you to quickly get back to a file you were working on without having to navigate into your documents or other folders to find it.

Before the digital age, when library books had checkout cards in the back, those paper cards were used to keep track of certain information about the book they were associated with. When a book was checked out, the checkout card would be filed away so that the library could know who checked that book out, and when they did so.

The purpose of the checkout card is to store information about something else. You can think of a Link file in much the same way. A library card is used to store information about where the book is located, who is in possession of the book, when the book was checked out, and other information. A Link file is the digital equivalent to a library card, storing information such as the location of the file it is associated with, the time that file was created, when it was last accessed, when it was last modified, and to which user account that file belongs.

However, there will be instances where you need to explain something more complicated with a level of detail that is not suited to a single graphic. In these instances, it is best to include a series of graphics in a presentation that build on one another to explain the concept or evidence in a case. We will look at examples of explaining more technically complicated explanations, aided by graphics, in this chapter.

CASE EXAMPLE: COMPLEX TECHNICAL EXPLANATION

The following presentation in this example was used with great success in a case I worked on, and this presentation was created specifically for this particular case. I was hired as an independent expert by the attorney who was representing the defendant. According to the opposing experts in this case, the defendant was in possession of contraband files.

In many cases, the mere existence of files on a computer that someone should not possess is enough for the opposing side to make a case. However, the attorney in my case understood that there is a difference between having something on your computer, and knowingly possessing that item on your computer.

Think of it this way; do you know all the files on your computer at this very moment? How about every single item in your house?

Do you know, with absolute certainty, that the last house guest you had made sure to collect every single piece of clothing, phone charger, candy wrapper, or other items they brought in with them? Probably not. Think of that same scenario, and then complicate it many, many times over and it would then be consistent with the case we are about to examine.

Computers contain many thousands of files. In this case, the contraband files only existed inside of one single file. On the computer hard drive running the Windows Vista operating system, there was a Macrium disk image, and buried inside of that Macrium disk image was a ZIP file, which is a compound file that can contain other files in a compressed format. Inside of that ZIP file were the handful of contraband files.

Explaining this scenario to a technical person with words alone can be complicated enough; now imagine trying to explain this with words only to laypeople on a jury. Well, this is where the power of illustrations comes in. We will examine the graphics slide by slide in the following presentation, and I am confident you will recognize how much easier it is to translate the complicated technical concepts efficiently and simply with graphics.

This example is where we will truly see why multiple graphics are often needed to explain more technical concepts. When dealing with laypersons, it is important to explain everything you need (without adding unnecessary complexity), with individual blocks of information building into the whole.

We have seen the following graphic before, and that is not by accident. The filing cabinet as file system is extremely helpful in my experience in aiding laypeople with the understanding of how data is generally organized on computer systems.

Plain Language Slide Explanation: On the computer hard drive is an operating system. The operating system on this particular computer is Windows XP. You can think of the data on your hard drive as a filing cabinet. Your operating system is the filing cabinet. Inside of that filing cabinet are partitions, such as C partition and D partition. These are the individual drawers of the filing cabinet. Inside of these drawers are individual folders. For example, your folders such as "My Documents," "My Pictures," and "My Music" would be inside of the C partition. Inside of the folders, such as "My Music," would be individual files. The files inside of the "My Music" folder would be the individual song files of your favorite artists.

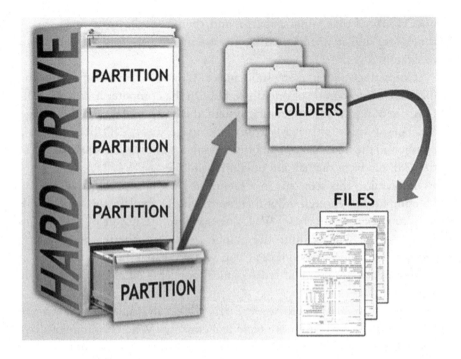

Now that we have explained how data is organized on a hard drive, we need to explain the next technical issue in this case, compound files. There are a number of points we need to make when explaining compound files, including their purpose, which is to compress numerous files into a single file both for convenient archiving and transmission. We also need to explain that unless browsed, a user cannot determine what is inside of a ZIP file. Of particular interest from this case example was the fact that the ZIP file was never decompressed, or extracted, on any of the computers (virtual or otherwise) in this case.

We are going to use our slide to convey the main point. We do not need the slide to explain every aspect of compression ratios and types related to compound files. The only pertinent information we need to transfer to our audience is that you cannot see the files inside of a ZIP file unless you do something with it.

Plain Language Slide Explanation: If I brought a backpack into your home and set it down, you would know that a backpack was now there, but you would not know what was inside of it. There could be one item inside, a dozen, or even hundreds of items. This is because the purpose of the backpack is to carry many things inside of one thing, the backpack.

A ZIP does the same thing digitally. It allows for many files to be placed into a single container and moved all at once in a convenient package.

You would not know what was inside of my backpack unless you unzipped the compartments and browsed through its contents. Once again, this is the same with the ZIP file. Unless the files inside of the ZIP file are looked at individually, a computer user does not know what is inside.

With my backpack, I could have a patch on the outside that says "Backpack full of cookies," but the inside could actually be filled with rat poison. With a ZIP file, the file could be named anything, "Pictures of Puppies," for instance, but all of the picture files inside could actually be of cats.

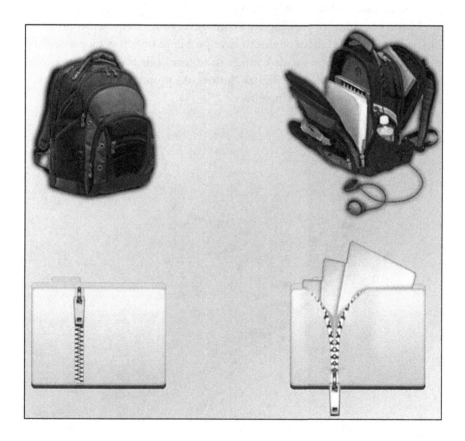

We then need to explain what a disk image is. In this case, the program used to make the disk images was Macrium Reflect. The way the program was used in this case was to create Macrium. MRIMG (Mirror Image) files of entire hard drives for backup purposes. Macrium develops tools for complete disaster recovery in case of catastrophic hardware failure. Once again we want to keep the explanation as simple and concise as possible, so we are going to explain to the court the main issue as it relates to the case; this disk image is basically an entire computer contained inside of a single file.

Plain Language Slide Explanation: If you could take your entire home and everything inside of it, make an exact copy, and shrink it down to fit inside of a single box that would do great in case if there was ever a disaster and your home was damaged or destroyed. You could then just unpack your magic box, and your home and all of your things would be there just as if the disaster had never happened.

That is the point of creating a disk image. If your computer stops working because the hard drive begins to have problems or you get a particularly nasty virus, you can use the disk image to restore your computer back to its original condition. All your digital "home and property" are safely duplicated and saved inside of a single file.

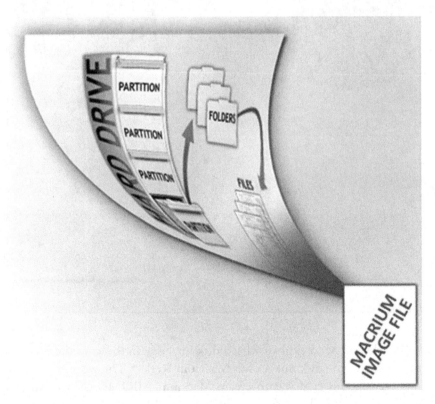

We then need to go back to the filing cabinet example we saw earlier, but this time, the files contained in the folders are of the Macrium disk images. In this case, there were multiple disk images inside of a folder. Only one of the multiple disk images contained the ZIP file with contraband in it. The rest were completely empty.

It was important in this case to note that there were numerous disk image files because inside of each image was a computer, further increasing the difficulty of actually knowing everything that was contained inside of each one. In reality, we may only have one computer that is of interest, but that one computer holds inside of it numerous other computers contained in disk images.

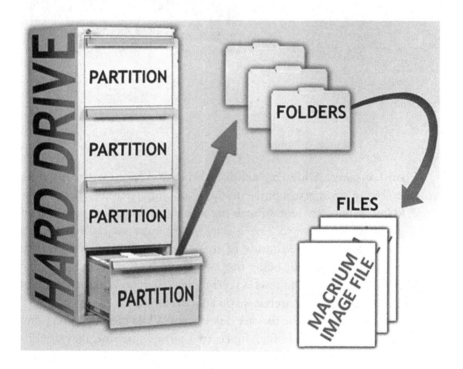

Plain Language Slide Explanation: Returning to our filing cabinet, we can see that inside of a folder are Macrium disk image files. Remember, each Macrium image file contains the contents of an entire computer.

We then need to explain what it would actually take for someone to be able to even get access to the data contained inside of the disk image file containing the ZIP file with the contraband images inside of it. It was claimed by the opposing side that the disk image file could be opened as a virtual machine as it existed on the defendant's computer. This was incorrect, as the disk image would have to be converted to a virtual machine first.

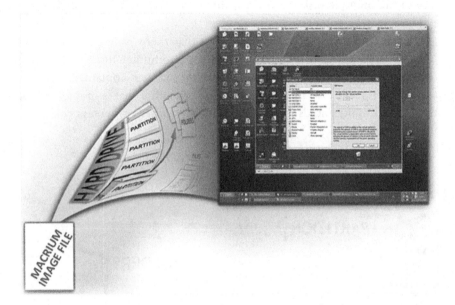

Plain Language Slide Explanation: When you have a virtual machine, you are able to open a computer inside of a computer using special software. Many technology professionals use virtual machines as a part of their work. It allows for them to have a single computer that can open many other computers contained inside of single virtual machine files on that one computer. The benefit being that you could have one computer that has virtual machines of Windows XP, Windows Vista, and Windows 7 to test your software products or websites you are developing.

In this case, however, the files are disk images. While they are a computer contained inside of a single file, similar to a virtual machine, they are different. And the main difference as it relates to this case is that they cannot be opened using virtual machine software without having another special program to convert the disk image into a virtual machine.

There is no program on the defendant's computer that would allow him/her to convert the disk image into a virtual machine, so he/she could not open the disk image containing the ZIP file with the contraband files inside on this computer at all.

We have made it clear that the disk image could not have been accessed by the defendant using virtual machine software. Instead, he/she would have to actually restore that disk image onto a new hard drive. Anyone with even a modicum of information technology experience will know that restoring a disk image to a hard drive is harder than just copying that data over to a new hard drive and installing it into a new computer. Issues related to the hardware in the computer, drivers for all of that hardware, and many other compatibility issues come into play. But as we have tried with every slide, we are going to keep the main thing the main thing and not delve into the rest.

The main thing for this slide is simple. The defendant did not have any other computer to restore the disk image onto in the first place.

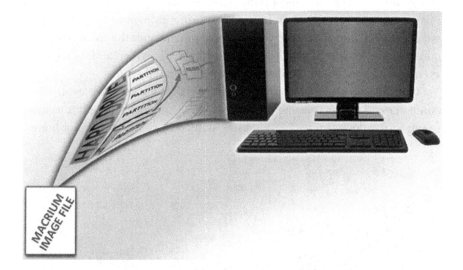

Plain Language Slide Explanation: The way the disk image was made in this case means that it could not be opened with virtual machine software. In other words, the "computer" contained within the disk image file could not be opened with special software inside of the defendant's computer. Instead, this disk image would have to be restored onto an entirely new hard drive. This means that he/she would either have to buy a new hard drive, or have one available, restore the disk image onto that hard drive, and place that hard drive inside of a computer that he/she had available or purchased. The data inside of this disk image is not something he/she, or anyone else, would have been able to access whenever they wanted to, as the process to even get access to the contraband files contained in the ZIP file on the disk image would require hours of work to access them.

At this point we have gotten through much of the technical information that it is critical to explain. Now we need to give our audience more perspective on how deeply buried within the computer's file system these contraband files actually were. In my experience, having testified dozens of times as an expert witness in digital forensics, even the information we have given so far, which has been clearly explained, will be fuzzy in the minds of some. This is not a criticism on the intelligence of a jury, but simply an understanding that some people are not engaged with or not interested in technology. The information we are trying to explain is so far outside of their normal experience that it needs to be explained in multiple ways using real-life examples that they can easily grasp.

We have laid the technical framework, explaining compound files, disk images, and file systems. Now it is time to bring it down to the lowest level we can, and making sure that the audience understands the main point; the contraband files were buried deep and there is no evidence the defendant even knew about them, let alone opened or accessed them.

This slide is our different layers at the 10,000 foot level. We explain our computer and files as containers (boxes) this time, using this metaphor to drive to our final slides when we introduce the warehouse to drive the point home.

Plain Language Slide Explanation: A computer contains data, and so does a disk image file. As we have discussed, a disk image is a file containing an entire computer. A Zip file is also a container, which holds individual files. We can think of each one of these as a box. The contents of the box will be the data stored inside of the computer, disk image, and Zip file, respectively.

We need the audience to understand at this point that the ZIP file is buried deep in the file system, so let's stack them inside one another.

Plain Language Slide Explanation: The ZIP file with the contraband files contained inside of it is buried deep on the computer system. Think of Matryoshka dolls, often called Russian nesting dolls, where we have a series of wooden dolls of decreasing size nested inside of each other. Each time you remove a doll, there is another inside, just smaller. The contraband files in this case would be inside of the smallest doll so to speak, they would not be on the outside for everyone to see. Looking at our slide, the contraband would be inside of the smallest box, the ZIP file, but this does not adequately explain how buried the contraband files are.

Continuing with our boxes, we are now going to enter the warehouse. I am confident all of our previous slides will make sense in the grand scheme now that we have gotten near the end of our presentation.

We need to explain that there are hundreds of thousands, if not millions, of individual files on a computer in this slide, as we will be introducing the disk image and ZIP files following this graphic.

Plain Language Slide Explanation: Think of your computer as a warehouse. Inside of that warehouse are boxes, and these boxes represent the files on your computer. If the warehouse in this slide was yours, would you feel that you truly knew the contents of each box? I know I would not. To know the contents of each box and be held accountable for those contents would be daunting, but the number of boxes in this warehouse is tiny compared to the number of files on your computer.

We then need to introduce the disk image file into our warehouse.

Plain Language Slide Explanation: In our warehouse of boxes, there is one particular box that is the disk image file. It is the glowing box left of center in the slide. Only one box inside of the warehouse of files contains contraband. But then we need to account for the ZIP file box, inside of that box.

Now we include the ZIP file as the smaller glowing box inside of the glowing box to drive home the "nesting" of that ZIP file containing the contraband as we previously described, just this time inside the "warehouse of files."

Plain Language Slide Explanation: You see, the ZIP file box is inside of the disk image file box, which is inside of the warehouse. If you are unsure of your ability to identify all of the boxes inside of a warehouse this size, how about the boxes nested inside of each of the boxes inside of the warehouse? These nested boxes could increase the total number of boxes you could be held accountable for "knowing about" by a dramatic amount.

But even the example from our last slide does not do justice to the scenario in this case, and now we get to what the entire presentation has been leading to. We have to explain that the contraband files, contained in a ZIP file, are inside of a computer file system, contained in a single disk image file, which is itself contained on the defendant's laptop's file system. We have a handful of contraband files, contained in a box, contained in a warehouse inside of a single box, which is contained inside of another warehouse.

Plain Language Slide Explanation: Working from the outside in, we have our warehouse first. This represents the defendant's computer. This is a warehouse with tens of thousands of files inside of it. Only one of those files is the disk image file in question. What we need to make sure to understand is that the disk image file is another entire warehouse of tens of thousands of files. Inside of the disk image warehouse is a single ZIP file. Inside of that ZIP file are a handful of contraband files.

SUMMARY

At this point we have explained to the jury that the defendant would have to go through many steps to access the contraband files; it is clearly understood by all who would view such a presentation that these files were not in plain sight, not readily searchable, or otherwise easy to locate or access. These facts, coupled with other technical information in the case, show that there was no evidence of the contraband ever being opened or accessed was used by his/her attorney to aid in a good outcome for the defendant.

In this chapter we have looked at a complicated example from a real case that benefited greatly from illustrations in explaining technical issues in plain language to laypersons in a way that understands that they may lack the technical background to readily understand the material, but also respects their intelligence. With our explanations, it is important to remember that when acting as a subject–matter expert we must explain things as clearly and as simply as possible. If our audience is unable to understand the concept we are attempting to convey, we have likely failed at communicating in the most beneficial form. A good idea of how to explain a technical concept in plain language, a great metaphor or analogy, is really able to shine in many instances with the inclusion of an excellent illustration.

CHAPTER SEVEN

Preparing Graphics for Production

Contents

Abstract

This chapter explains basic production components of graphics, as well as covering real-world issues that can take place when preparing graphics and presentations for the courtroom.

Keywords: Expert testimony; Graphic design; Presentation; Printing; Resolution.

Information in this chapter:

- Limitations and benefits of print and digital presentation mediums
- Quick guide on how to prepare flexible graphics for production
- Other considerations for presenting graphics in court

INTRODUCTION

After going through the hard work of creating just the right graphics to explain the technical concept in your case, there is still one important step to consider before you are done. Just because that graphic looks great on your computer monitor does not mean it will look great in the final form it takes on. This is why the final step of preparing visuals for production can be so critical. This is especially true when dealing with graphics that will be used in court. Sometimes you have the full range of capabilities

Digital Forensics Trial Graphics
ISBN 978-0-12-803483-5
http://dx.doi.org/10.1016/B978-0-12-803483-5.00007-4

in a courtroom such as projectors or big screen high-definition televisions. Other times you are constrained to displaying your graphics onto plain old pieces of printer paper in black and white.

With these potential issues in mind, we will examine in this chapter how to prepare our graphics for both print and digital mediums. We will also examine how to prepare visuals in such a way that they work well for both mediums at the same time in case you are limited to one form or another in the courtroom. Our goal is that whatever the final form the graphic takes, print or digital, that the information is conveyed clearly and concisely without any detraction due to the final medium of delivery.

There are thousands of books and websites that explain with great detail how to prepare print and digital graphics. You can easily find that information elsewhere. To reiterate in different words, the point of this chapter is to provide real-world advice garnered from experience in courtrooms and from giving hundreds of presentations. If you want to learn how to perfectly replicate colors or design business cards then I suggest you seek out a book that trains you to be a graphic designer. Our objective is to make you proficient in graphic design as a means to an end; translating complicated technical concepts in plain language to laypeople.

UNDERSTANDING LIMITATIONS

You can be anything you want when you grow up; I am not talking about those kinds of limitations. What we are concerned about here is specifically related to using graphics at trial. Having testified as an expert in many different courtrooms, I can attest that the technological capabilities in different courthouses range from archaic to relatively modern.

With that in mind, let's look at some limitations we are likely to have in print and digital mediums, examine some practical considerations, and then dive into the details.

Print

The benefits of printed graphics, if you are the one who is actually in charge of printing or getting the graphics printed, is that you know what the final product looks like as it will be displayed in court before you ever get there. Other benefits include the ability to make multiple copies of the graphic so that, for example, every member of a jury could review the graphic at the same time (and if the graphic has been entered into evidence, they could potentially have it available in the jury room during deliberation).

While there are numerous benefits to print, there are downsides as well. First, you may be constrained to only black and white instead of using full color. This is especially problematic if the original graphic you designed was created with the intention to only be viewed in full color. An example would be a graphic that explains multiple points, or delineates multiple subjects on a graphic in different colors. When that color graphic is viewed in black and white it can become muddied.

While it might seem far-fetched that you would be forced to print a color graphic in black and white, I have had multiple instances where I have flown in the night before, found out a graphic was needed in court for my testimony the next day, and had to print my graphic or report that contained full color graphics in black and white at the hotel business center.

I have also had occasions where a graphic or section of a report I have written was printed by the attorney who retained me, or opposing counsel, in black and white and I had to use that for my explanations on the stand. While I might mention during testimony that the original graphic was in color, I would not want that issue to impede my testimony or be a distraction to a jury.

The second primary issue with print is that you are more constrained by size. The size of the graphic you can create is dependent on the largest printer you have access to, or the largest printer that funds allow. Large-scale printing can be expensive and is not always an option. If you have a detailed road map of user activity portrayed in a single graphic, printing it on standard printer paper is probably going to be counterproductive versus printing it on a large poster board.

The finality of print also needs to be taken into consideration. If there is a mistake on the final printed product, it cannot be changed without first fixing it on a computer and then printing it again. If we are talking about printing the graphic on a large poster board that entails considerable time, effort, and cost. This might not be an option given time or location constraints when the rubber hits the road.

Despite the drawbacks of printed material, it is beneficial that you don't need a computer, projector, or television to show it to someone. You can just pull the printed graphic out of your briefcase. Because of this, I would suggest always having a backup copy of your graphic in printed form, even if you intend to use a television or projector to show the graphic. As someone who uses technology every day, I recommend a degree of healthy skepticism concerning it working when and how you need it to.

Digital

Having your graphics in digital format means that you can transport them on a USB stick in your pocket, and display the graphic in its full glory on a screen or television. Of course, this means that we are assuming everything works as intended when you get to your presenting location or courtroom.

I give presentations across the United States, primarily to attorneys, and I can tell you from experience that graphics in digital format are awesome when they work, and they usually do, but I have had enough instances where there were serious complications that I always have some form of printed backup.

One instance where I trusted too much in technology was at a conference for attorneys where I was on a panel of experts answering questions, and then was supposed to immediately go from there into a PowerPoint presentation. In this instance there was no time to solve a technical issue. I needed to be able to plug in a USB into the computer they provided, open my presentation, and begin. I naively expected their provided computer to work as advertised, which of course, it did not. I ended up giving my 30 min presentation without any slides.

I have many examples when adapters, interfaces, and a myriad of other issues made connecting a laptop to whatever projection system was available in the courtroom, hotel, or convention center made for difficult times. Unless you travel with your own complete setup from laptop to projector everywhere you go, and you are allowed to use your own gear at the speaking location, you will encounter similar issues. Many courtrooms wouldn't allow you to even bring that kind of gear inside. As a side note, this is why I recommend always getting to your speaking engagement at least 30 min early to scope out the projector or television you will be connecting to in case there are technical problems.

Even if all the technology works perfectly issues can still arise. One such instance happened to me when I was a speaker at one of the largest annual digital forensics conferences. At this conference you send in your presentation well in advance so that all the technical bugs are worked out by a professional audio/video company. All a speaker has to do is show up and start their presentation. I arrived at the room I was assigned to early as is my habit. After looking around inside the podium, under the table runner, and inside the audio/video cart, it became apparent that there was no computer in the room. I called the company in charge of the audio/video equipment and they sent one of their technicians over immediately. Apparently, the computer had been stolen! Luckily, the audio/video company was able to get another computer and get me up and running seconds before I was scheduled to start.

I share these stories because I want you to be prepared whenever you go to present. Make sure you know your graphics, whether it is a single illustration or an entire presentation. Never assume you'll have a chance to run through your slides before you get there, and never assume the technology is actually going to work when you get there. Always have a backup plan; as the saying goes, "hope for the best, but prepare for the worst."

QUICK GUIDE TO PREPARING GRAPHICS

In your mind's eye is the perfect graphic to illustrate a concept for the courtroom. Now it is time to make that idea a reality. An understandable first reaction is the question, "where do I start?" The following guide is designed to help you avoid creating a finished graphic that has some sort of major deficiency when you get to the final product. Have you ever purchased a piece of furniture that was "some assembly required" and at the end had a handful of unused parts and pieces? I sure have. This can often be the by-product of poor planning (or poor instructions). This quick guide will help you end up with a satisfactory final product, a sturdy piece of furniture instead of a wobbly one.

Canvas

Canvas is an old term. You have probably heard it associated with painting or the sails on a sailboat. As with most terminology related to technology, it is used to give a framework to understand a technical concept with a commonly understood physical object. Think about it, the main screen on your computer is your "desktop." There is no desk, let alone a desktop, on your computer (Fig. 7.1).

First things first, what are you preparing your graphic for? Is it for print or the projector? This is going to help you determine what size to make your canvas. The default canvas for Photoshop is 8.5 by 11 in, the size of standard printer paper. Many times people will just use this default canvas size even when making graphics that will be projected. The problem is that if you take the graphic designed on a canvas meant for a piece of paper, it will likely look grainy, distorted, and fuzzy if stretched to fit a big screen TV or projector. Try to make your canvas size the same as the screen, projector, or paper that the graphic will be presented on. If you're not sure what you will be presenting on, I suggest keeping with a standard aspect ratio (Figs. 7.2 and 7.3).

It is almost always a good idea to go from larger to smaller if you intend to use the graphic in multiple formats. Design the graphic for the projector first, with an appropriately sized canvas. Then for the version that will be printed, just shrink the graphics to fit accordingly. When you shrink

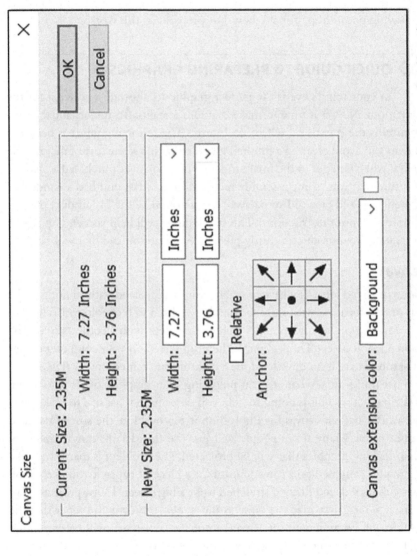

Figure 7.1 This is the "Canvas Size" settings option within Adobe Photoshop. Graphic design programs such as Photoshop use legacy terminology from photography and painting that predates the digital age.

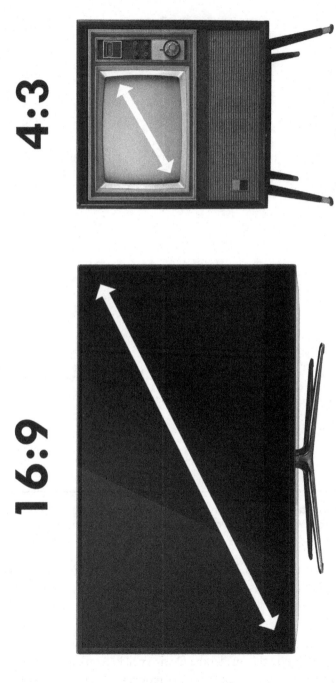

Figure 7.2 If you think your graphic will be presented on a modern TV or projector, use 16:9. If you think it will be on older equipment, you might want to opt for 4:3.

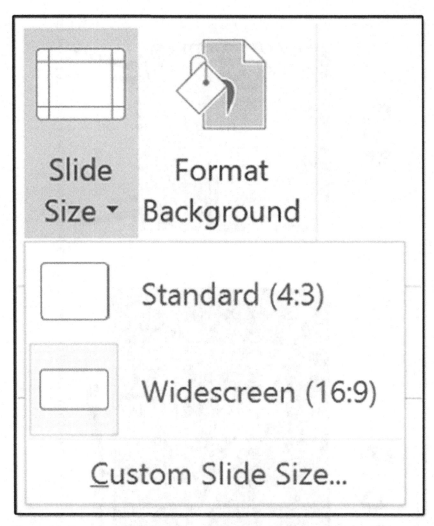

Figure 7.3 Presentation programs typically have this in the default options. This screenshot is from Microsoft PowerPoint, under the "Slide Size" menu option.

graphics you don't lose quality like you do when enlarging them. This is largely a by-product of resolution, which is our next topic.

Resolution

The higher the resolution of a graphic, the bigger the file size will be. Conversely, the lower the resolution the smaller the file size will be. You can always optimize a graphic to make it smaller, but you can't retroactively add resolution. When creating your graphic you want the original to be high resolution (Fig. 7.4).

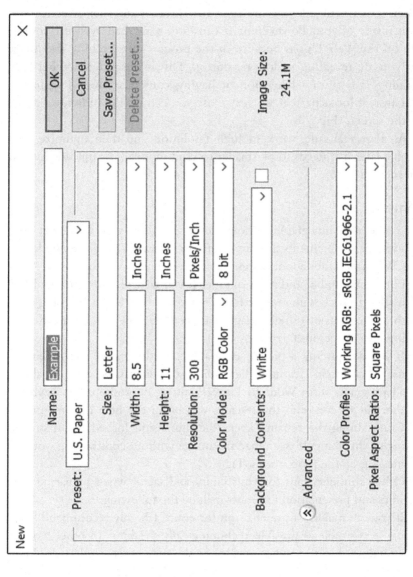

Figure 7.4 When creating your canvas, a good ratio of pixels per inch (resolution) is 300. The more the pixels per inch (the higher the number), the higher the resolution.

If you watch a show on a television that is not high definition you will immediately notice how poor the picture quality is versus modern high definition televisions. This is because the resolution is significantly lower. Most of us have experienced this when dealing with graphics too. When you download a picture from the Internet and then stretch it out to fit inside of your PowerPoint, it can look really bad even if it looked fine on the Web. This is because in the process of stretching the image out you are revealing its low resolution. This is the difference between standing 10 ft from a television or having your face pressed against it; 10 ft away it looks perfect, up very close you can see the individual pixels on the screen (Fig. 7.5).

As a general rule, work in high resolution and then optimize your graphic later if it needs to be smaller to send in emails or uploaded to the Internet (Fig. 7.6).

Content

The content of your graphic is going to be specific to your needs; but there are some design elements that are helpful to follow for purely aesthetic reasons. When in doubt about design choices, remember the following:

- Limit the number and types of fonts. If you have text in your graphic, it is safest to stick with a single font, sometimes two. If you are using more than two fonts in a single image, you are either a design expert or crossing into dangerous territory.
- If you are placing a picture or graphic on the canvas and resizing it, use a "constrain" feature when doing so. This can be done in almost all programs from Word to PowerPoint to Photoshop. The keyboard shortcut to constrain the resizing will be in the help documentation. Constraining the resizing keeps the dimension locked when stretching or shrinking. If you resize the image without constraining, you risk messing up the proportions (Fig. 7.7).

Other considerations for your sanity and safety when preparing your graphics and presentation for court include the following:

- If you are making a presentation for court, I highly recommend keeping it as simple as possible, technologically speaking. In other words, I would not include audio or video in the presentation unless absolutely necessary. Increased complexity makes it more likely for something to go wrong. It is never fun to have to fix a technical glitch in the middle of a presentation.

Figure 7.5 The unappealing outcome of overstretching a small graphic.

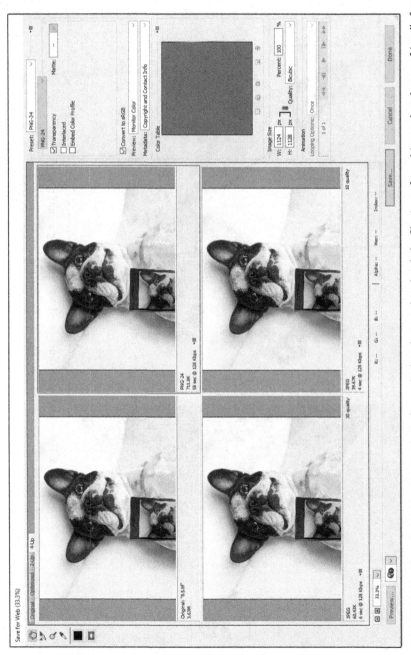

Figure 7.6 This is the "Save for Web" option in Photoshop, which is designed to shrink the file sizes of graphics so that they are friendly for the Internet. Almost all graphic design programs have similar features.

freeform stretch

constrain stretch

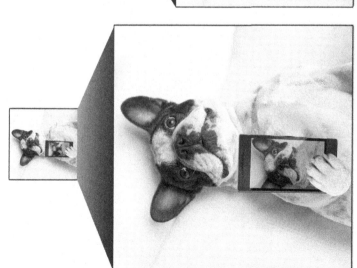

Figure 7.7 This difference between a "constrain" stretch and a "freeform" stretch.

- Know the graphic. Imagine the scenario where your graphic is printed on paper. There is only one copy of the graphic, and an attorney is showing it to the jury with a document camera. Everyone can clearly see the graphic but you, the expert on the witness stand can't. From your perspective it is difficult to see. You should be able to explain the graphic from your mind's eye with words only, and without the aid of the graphic itself, a laser pointer, or need to point at the image in any way.
- Test your graphic before presenting it. Make sure that it looks how you want when it is projected, on a television, or printed. Make sure your graphic looks great on all of these mediums in case you have to go to plan B because of circumstances outside of your control.

SUMMARY

In this chapter we looked at why it is important to create your graphic in such a way that it can be used in numerous mediums, from print to presentations. We took a high level view at the most important design elements related to producing graphics capable of crossing mediums, and how to be prepared for any scenario with backup plans on presenting your material.

APPENDIX A: RESOURCES FOR BETTER PRESENTATIONS

7 DESIGN TIPS ON HOW TO MAKE AN EFFECTIVE, BEAUTIFUL POWERPOINT PRESENTATION

http://www.shutterstock.com/blog/tips-on-how-to-make-effective-beautiful-powerpoint-presentations.

DESIGN RESOURCES BY CANVA

https://designschool.canva.com/design-resources/.

CANVA DESIGN SCHOOL

https://designschool.canva.com.

CANVA DESIGN SCHOOL RESOURCES

https://designschool.canva.com/design-resources/.

THE ETHOS3 BLOG: PRESENTATION TIPS AND TRICKS

https://www.ethos3.com/blog/.

SHUTTERSTOCK

http://www.shutterstock.com/home.

ISTOCK PHOTOS

http://www.istockphoto.com.

GARR REYNOLDS—PRESENTATION TIPS

http://www.garrreynolds.com/preso-tips/.

SLIDE:OLOGY BY NANCY DUARTE. THE ART AND SCIENCE OF CREATING GREAT PRESENTATIONS

http://www.duarte.com/book/slideology/.

DUARTE.COM YOUTUBE CHANNEL

https://www.youtube.com/user/duartedesign/featured.

BEYOND BULLET POINTS—CLIFF ATKINSON'S WEB SITE

http://beyondbulletpoints.com.

GARR REYNOLDS: WHAT IS GOOD PRESENTATION DESIGN?

http://presentationzen.blogs.com/presentationzen/2005/09/whats_good_powe.html.

CRAIG BALL'S POWER PERSUASION

http://www.craigball.com/PowerPersuasion_2011.pdf.

INDEX

Printed in the United States
By Bookmasters